INTUITIVE CLAIRVOYANCE

2023

Robert Mason

Introduction........
Chapter One...   Spiritual gifts learning clairvoyance
Chapter Two ...... Spiritual Research X Project
Chapter Three......Spiritual Development Ps 25 - 46

Chapter Four ...... How Angels interact with us

Chapter Five......... Aspects of the Soul

Chapter Six .... Angels at work

Chapter Seven...... Premonitions

Chapter Eight ...... Angels Communication

Chapter Nine ...... Angels can give us visions

Chapter Ten .... Our Guardian Angels know our future

Chapter Eleven ... Discovering the meaning of life

Chapter Twelve.... First Heaven

Chapter Thirteen...The Past and Future are linked

Chapter Fourteen... Life as a person seeing Angels

Copyright Robert Mason 2023

INTRODUCTION

My name is Robert Mason. I am a clairvoyant, medium and psychic. In the past twenty years I have given many thousands of readings. When I was younger I wasn't clairvoyant. I opened up a latent clairvoyant gift inadvertently through my spiritual research. I believe that some people have a clairvoyant ability that is suppressed and they don't realise they have a gift. Many more people have some degree of clairvoyant ability. Following the same path as I did, I now teach people how to discover, understand, and gradually open up their clairvoyant and psychic abilities. I call the teachings "Intuitive Clairvoyance ".Learning clairvoyance is safe and good because I teach a clairvoyant ability that connects to Heaven. The learning path can be positively life changing in a way that leads to future life fulfilment. Quiet miracles can happen! Join me on this amazing spiritual journey!

Why Learn Intuitive Clairvoyance?

1) It is a foundation level clairvoyance that many people can achieve

2) A gradually acquired knowingness that we have a soul and that there is an afterlife, reducing fear of our mortality

3) An increasing awareness of our Guardian Angels

4) Learning to identify negative spiritual energies, negative influences, and paranormal phenomena, knowing exactly what they are and how to deal with it.

5) We may find ourselves receiving premonitions

6) Discovering some of the meaning of life in a way that satisfies our logic

7) Discovering spiritual healing help via the Angels for ourselves and to help others

8) A greater communication flow from our Guardian Angels into our intuitive feelings. They guide us every day of our lives. I teach thought projection, for this is the way that we communicate with Heaven.

9) A foundation in psychic ability.

10) A true path of spiritual growth and life fulfilment.

11) Helping others, using your spiritual gifts.

Help make the world a better place! The spiritual knowledge that I teach describes working with our Guardian Angels from Heaven. My personal mediumship gift is enabled by the Guardian Angels who bring messages from loved ones who have made it safely across to Heaven and are spiritually ALIVE in Heaven. We may begin to see how Heaven brings healing to life, nature and the environment. We can truly become aware of our individual purpose in helping others and helping nature and the environment heal and survive. I believe if many more people can learn to be intuitively guided by our Guardian Angels, then humanity and life in nature stands a better chance of survival in the century ahead.

Foundation teachings

Firstly, satisfying our logical mind that we can allow ourselves spiritual beliefs. Personal spiritual experience that helps create beliefs that over-rides logic. This could be feelings inside, a personal spiritual experience. OR a mediumship/ psychic reading

Explaining the System and all about our Guardian Angels. Learning the system of the meaning of life, First Heaven, and Guardian Angels. Intuitive clairvoyance only connects with Heaven and the Guardian Angels.

Teaching concerning the different negative energies and paranormal phenomena.

Developing our intuitive senses, feelings, and sudden knowingness. I give real life accounts of people experiencing intuitive guidance and warnings. Aspects of the Soul. Premonitions.

Communicating with Heaven via thought projection

Sensing Healing energies. FEEL their colours. SENSE their colours. Then begin to SEE their colours. Healing others means projecting unconditional love, if only for the time of healing.

Finally, tuition of the personal qualities we need to become fully clairvoyant with a gift of mediumship. However, such a gift is only fully granted by Heaven.

Hold or acquire a belief in our spritualuality
We need to convince our logical mind that we are spiritual, and that there is an afterlife. This can happen if we have been through a personal spiritual experience such as a Near Death Experience, through a mediumship or psychic reading, and by learning the amazing facts concerning the Meaning of Life that I teach. Some or all, of the knowledge may fit with your personal beliefs.

Learn about First Heaven – our true home

Discovering that Guardian Angels are real
Learning about our Guardian Angels as our link with Heaven. Learning how they communicate through our intuitive feelings and sudden knowingness.

Learning how we can communicate with them through thought

projection.

I only teach intuitive clairvoyance that is enabled by our Guardian Angels. This is safe, because we only connect with Heaven, and unconditional love.

Learn about negative energies - the opposite of Love
Learning about negative energies. Negative earthbound energies. Learn about the paranormal and how to deal with such phenomena. How to protect ourselves from negative energies.

Discover your true-life plan
We all have a Life Plan, determined in Heaven before we were born. Learn to discover your Life Plan and being guided by your Guardian Angel to regain your true path to life fulfilment.

Personal Qualities
Are you never self-centred? Do you have empathy for others? Learn the personal qualities that we need to gain an intuitive clairvoyant gift. We are working with our Guardian Angels who decide if we can handle intuitive clairvoyance responsibly. I describe the different Aspects of the Soul later in this book.

Spiritual energies from Angels

When we start to spiritually grow, we can begin to sense these energies and see the colours of these energies as they flow through from the healing Angels. In personal tuition I teach how to sense, feel and SEE these energies.

What is the outcome of learning Intuitive Clairvoyance?

Helping someone become more spiritually intuitive is a form of life coaching that motivates people towards their true goals and desired self.

We can work out the best way forward through our problems in life with intuitive insights.

Becoming spiritually intuitive generates a true connection with the Guardian Angels, mainly our personal Guardian Angel

True intuitive abilities help us to help ourselves and others through life with personal life situations

We may receive premonitions of the future with a fully developed intuitive ability

We can learn to sense the Healing Angels and sense, see, and feel their spiritual healing energies for ourselves and others.

The following is a true account of how our Guardian Angels may try to warn us by giving us strong intuitive feelings.

Grandad Alan had recently passed at age eighty-one years. His granddaughter told me that he had almost suffered a tragic fate many years earlier. He worked as a fishing hand on a Hull trawler when he was younger. One day he arrived at the dock to board his trawler when he had an overwhelming feeling of something wrong. The feeling was so strong that he went home instead of going out to sea. He had worked on the same trawler for several years and never felt this way before. When he arrived home his wife wasn't happy because they needed the income, but he couldn't shake off the feelings that something might happen to the trawler. Several days later it was reported that the trawler had disappeared, feared lost at sea. The trawler never returned and was never found. All the fishing crew had died.

Many people experience intuitive feelings. Perhaps a feeling that someone isn't telling the truth. Perhaps feelings that we shouldn't take a certain course of action or take a journey to a certain place. As a spiritual researcher I set out many years ago to discover the meaning of life, a meaning to life. As a part of my research, I sought to find out where intuitive feelings come from. I realise that such feelings are often generated by our brain. These feelings can be brought to the surface from our memory of past experiences. However, many people describe intuitive feelings that cannot be explained. They may feel as if there was something spiritual at work. Through my research I sought to discover what the "Something spiritual" is. To my surprise I discovered that not only do Angels and Guardian Angels exist, but they communicate with us through our intuitive feelings.

I only teach about Angels and Guardian Angels from what might be described as "Heaven". Such descriptions I disassociate from religious terms insofar as I can because my research conclusions are always based on logical assumptions.

Throughout this book I will present my research conclusions as a basis for my teachings, together with true accounts to support my narrative.

We live our physical lives as human beings on an Earth that is full of negative energies. Through lack of empathy for others and self-centred behaviour there is much suffering on Earth. We can stay safer and live more fulfilling lives if we start to recognise and trust intuitive guidance from our Guardian Angels. A necessary part of my teachings is to learn about the negative energies that manifest on Earth. In the following chapter I describe an account of how the most extreme paranormal phenomena can manifest. I also describe how we can deal with the paranormal, with help from our Guardian Angels.

CHAPTER ONE

Spiritual gifts learning clairvoyance

It is surprising how many people and families are troubled by ghosts and what seem to be evil spirits. Society around us doesn't accept such phenomena as real and so there is very little knowledge about what causes this phenomenon and how to deal with it. If we learn to sense the Angels, tune in to Heaven, then we have an infinite amount of the most powerful energies of Heaven at our disposal to correctly identify the paranormal phenomena. The following is a true account:
I was called to a beautiful modern detached home. A normal respectable businessman and his wife had heard of me, and my ability to remove hauntings. Their three children, one young man, and two girls were in their early teens and very clued-up on being cool and fashionable. They seemed to view my visit with cool indifference. Their mum was certainly not cool. She was stressed and at the end of her wits. She immediately started to pour out an explanation of what was happening. Every night she would awake, pinned to her bed so tightly that she couldn't speak by some invisible force that she knew was an evil spirit. Her husband never witnessed this, but always slept through these incidents in a deep relaxed sleep. He had not experienced any weird experiences. She described lights flashing on and off and electrical appliances switching on and off, always when her

husband was out. I spoke with the children who were not frightened but had heard footsteps on the stairs when no-one else was in the house, and all three had seen a ghost in the house, usually on the stairs. The ghost wasn't identifiable as male or female, but just a shadowy form.
Having listened to what they all had to say I firstly went to the stairway. There, hovering on the stairs was a grey mist. I knew this entity was the culprit, but what on earth was it? I then went down into the kitchen, directly beneath the stairs. I went alone. Confronting me was this grey mist, complete with a very scary head, menacing, and telling me to go. It was like a huge caterpillar, long, grey, hovering with this evil face in front of me. It was trying to scare me, but I was stronger. I knew this entity had been human at some time, but the person had been evil in life, and become so twisted in the afterlife as to completely lose its human identity. These things are depicted as fantasy in films that children watch. Our society is so misguided. These entities really exist and should not be taken lightly. I told the entity to go and leave this family alone. The entity became more frightening, came closer and gave a clear message that it was stopping where it was. For the first time I felt a shiver run up my spine. In the lounge I heard someone fall. A tough army friend of mine, a veteran of frontline fighting in Iraq, had been suddenly targeted by this spiritual energy, felt weird, very unwell, and collapsed. He had just come along out of genuine interest, but I feel also for his own amusement. He never expected this.
I had to think quickly and reverted to my Christian Faith. I spoke out loudly with a prayer to God. "In the name of Jesus Christ, I command you to go." The entity retreated. The solid walls of the house became transparent. I could still see this entity outside of the home, in the spiritual distance. "I pray to Father God to send the rescue Angels in to remove this entity." A beautiful Light appeared, and two Angels came out of the Light and grabbed the entity and took it away. My view of the scene became solid again, the walls of the house were now solid, and the entity gone. The atmosphere in the home had also, very suddenly, become normal, light, friendly, relaxed, and safe. I then asked my Angel Guide what had caused this evil entity to be in this house. I received a

response immediately, now seeing clearly that the house was built on what is called a "Ley Line". These are lines of invisible energy criss-crossing the earth that were of great significance to ancient peoples because it is on these lines that Stonehenge, and other ancient monoliths were built. They are lines of intense spiritual energy. You know what? the ley line from their house also went straight through a hospital at the top of their road that at one time had been a sanatorium for people with mental illness. The time-period of the sanatorium was around 100 years earlier. Quite a few lost souls were giving the residents of this new housing estate a scary time as I found out afterwards. I was subsequently called to clear several hauntings, both human and poltergeist, on this upmarket new housing estate. I feel sorry for others suffering such misery from evil spirits, or negative energy from misguided, lost souls. Many people suffer in silence, not knowing where to turn for help, and fearing that they will be ridiculed.

When I see children dressed like scary ghosts on Halloween, I don't find it child's play. I shudder and think "If only society, if only parents, knew the truth."

Most souls pass to a Heaven-like place at the end of life's days, even if they had no religious beliefs. It is quite common for the Guardian Angel of a recently passed soul to bring a sign to loved ones left behind. This is not paranormal negative energies at work but signs from Heaven.

The following true account is where a grandfather who was not able to work modern technology had a huge helping hand from his Guardian Angel after he passed.

Anne had helped her mother nurse her grandfather George, her mother's father, through a long period of illness. In his final weeks of life, he had been in hospital but had requested to be transferred home to spend his last days with his remaining family. The family home, as with many modern homes, has a voice activated internet search unit in the lounge.

Two days after her George's death, Anne came home from shopping, accompanied with her mother. The internet search unit had activated "Play music" which was sounding out loud as they entered their home. No-one else was in the building. The song it was playing was Grandfather George's favourite song. They were both bewildered and surprised and had no logical answers for why the music should be playing. The music was loud, and Anne's mother exclaimed, away from the voice activated unit in the kitchen: "This is too loud". To their further amazement the song immediately quietened.

Anne's sister, who lived elsewhere, phoned minutes later to say that music was playing in her home without her instruction. She was quite shocked by this and further amazed that the song the internet playing was the one chosen to play at the funeral service. "Could it be Grandfather George?" was the question the family asked themselves. "How could George be so clever as to manipulate a voice activated internet search device? He had suffered mild dementia prior to his death."

As a clairvoyant I later heard this account from Anne. My first thoughts were that this is explained by the technology because internet devices listen to our conversations. However, the house had been empty when the music started playing, and the same phenomena happening to the sister at the same time is difficult to explain logically. I asked the Angels concerning this incident and received immediate confirmation that the music playing in both households had been a sign from George that his soul had survived death. We are fully restored with our memories once we reach Heaven in our state as a soul. However, we are not clever enough to operate computer search engine devices in our soul state, but those in Heaven are. Heaven is the source of infinite intelligence, of all knowledge, and our Guardian Angels find it easy to help us because they access this knowledge.

Through learning spiritual intuition, we can learn to identify and recognise almost every type of paranormal phenomena. Although most souls who pass through to the afterlife don't cause paranormal phenomena, it is quite common prior to the funeral for a deceased soul to cause things to happen by way of a sign to say, "I have survived physical death". After the funeral such signs often cease.

CHAPTER TWO

Spiritual Research X

My name is Robert Mason. I am a spiritual researcher. I started a project called the "Spiritual Research X Project" in the year 1980. After many years of research, I reached a point where I had made significant discoveries concerning the meaning of life and whether we have a soul. I acquired knowledge providing evidence of our true spiritual nature, and that we each have a soul that is the "I am" or "Me" inside us. We survive physical death, and we retain our memories and our character as we pass back to the spiritual realm. I gradually built up my skills in perceiving spiritual energies and phenomena that manifest at the periphery of our sensual awareness. The skills acquired using my research discoveries subsequently led to an inadvertent outcome when I applied them in real-life situations. I realised that I had gained the wonderful life-changing gifts of clairvoyance, medium and psychic ability. I have since given many thousands of clairvoyant readings and I continue to give people readings that bring messages, including names, from loved ones who have passed. I also receive premonitions of the future. Furthermore, I have been able to continue my research, often receiving answers from those in the Afterlife. I have built up a picture of the meaning of life and gained an extraordinary understanding of the paranormal. Knowledge built up through research helps me identify and explain the spiritual reasons for almost every type of paranormal phenomena. The basic knowledge I have acquired is detailed in this book, along with real-life examples of how the different paranormal phenomena can be identified. I now teach people clairvoyance. This is learnt as a series of spiritual skills that are built on as we grow in our own spiritual development. Learning clairvoyance can be of real benefit when encountering paranormal phenomena. We can identify the type of paranormal phenomena, communicate with it, protect ourselves from it and deal with it.

Spiritual Research X discoveries are described as spiritual "Insights" and must make sense in a logical manner for those with an open mind to true spiritual understanding. Spiritual science is the science of a non-physical dimension. "Insight" conclusions cannot be proved by physical science. The spiritual dimension is not subject to laws of the physical universe.

The content of this book includes a description of the "Insights" derived from the discoveries concerning paranormal phenomena, who and what we really are as human beings, and the bigger picture concerning "What is life all about?". We are living in an age of fear contrasted by new enlightenment concerning spiritual truths. This enlightenment has been partly brought about by a huge improvement in the ways we communicate.

*Spiritual Research into the
existence of the human soul*

What is our soul?
Our soul is an energy made of the energy of the spiritual dimension. With our physical senses we are unable to detect any energies that are from other dimensions, and other dimensions

do exist as theorized in the science of quantum mechanics. We are unable to see, feel, touch, hear or smell our soul energy but that doesn't mean to say that our soul energy doesn't exist. It is very real and our soul, whom we really are, is a conscious energy of the spiritual dimension.

Our soul energy is a conscious energy. All energies move and behave in certain ways. We have the unique identity property within ourselves of the ultimate state of consciousness, the "I Am". We are intelligent and possess memory and character attributes. We are a part of the ultimate intelligence of all universes without which there would be no creation, no purpose, no ambition, no anything.

Ancient civilizations believed in spiritual entities and religions evolved

Throughout history, and dating back to the earliest civilizations, societies have held beliefs in an unseen spiritual dimension and that human beings have a soul. Perception of the truth seems to have been clouded by humans controlling others and spelling out their own version of religion, spiritual ceremonies, and rituals. However, if we are biological computers with no soul, it would be unlikely that human beings would have, so widely across different societies, continents and across different time periods, come up with the concept of an unseen spiritual dimension. There would have been no need for such a concept. Instead, human beings, without doubt, have consistently felt their spirituality and spiritual forces at work in nature. The ability for humans to have these feelings shows our spirituality as a major factor in understanding whom we are.

Human activity
Human activity offers overwhelming evidence of the human soul. If we had no soul and were nothing more than organic computers, we would not have any need to explore, seek adventure, and pursue new experiences. We would not seek entertainment or become bored when we have nothing interesting to do. The human soul expresses the person inside throughout life. Our art, music, literature and poetry are all expressions of the soul.

Emotions

Without a soul we would not feel emotions. Our brain may trigger the physical emotional reactions such as tears when we are sad or a raised voice when we are angry. However, it is our soul, the "I am" inside that triggers the brain.

There has been an upsurge in interest in ghost hunting and the paranormal, with many television programmes and films being produced by professional ghost hunting teams.

The reason for the upsurge in interest is that hauntings often create paranormal phenomena that can be picked up by the human senses and by scientific instruments. Ghost hunters may claim that they are seeking proof of an Afterlife and the continued existence of the human soul beyond physical death by trying to obtain evidence of paranormal activity.

Ghosts and poltergeists tend to create the most noticeable phenomena, yet such phenomena are only produced by a tiny minority of souls. Most souls seem to produce no phenomena after physical death, although some unusual phenomena in the form of "Signs" can be experienced within a week or so of death. We are a soul energy temporarily dwelling in the physical body of a human being. There are reasons that we are denied a conscious memory of existence in a place that might be called "Heaven" before birth. Our soul memory is deliberately blanked off before birth so that memories of our previous existence, such as a past life, do not interfere with our present life.

This research explains what happens to our soul after physical life and what phenomena can be detected.

The Human Brain

My research into the nature of the human brain from a spiritual perspective is important because the knowledge aids our understanding of paranormal phenomena.

Computers
It is only with the advent of the computer age, and the increased sophistication of computer memory, operating systems and software that we may allow ourselves to see the brain as a biological supercomputer.

Within the brain there are different areas that each have their own purpose. These include pre-programmed areas that control the function of the bodily organs, especially noticeable with the heart rate and lungs.

Other areas control our pre-programmed instinctive behaviors. We have parts of the brain that store long-term and short-term memory. These areas are not pre-programmed with ready-made memories. They are blank, almost like a blank computer memory drive, ready to accept new memories as we begin life's adventure.

Spiritual Beliefs
Religions generally preach that we each have a soul that is our true inner spiritual self. They also teach many different versions of a spiritual realm, as another dimension.

Within this book I accept that humanity throughout several thousand years of recorded history has almost consistently held spiritual beliefs. If we are just flesh and blood, then how can humanity hold the concepts and generate feelings of a spiritual dimension?

It can be logically concluded that within our brain is the place where our soul energy meets and joins with the biological computer of our brain.

The human brain has the extraordinary capability to act as a link between two dimensions of the spiritual and physical universes. What other organ, computer or machine on Earth has that capability?

As human beings our soul energy links so perfectly with our brain that we may forget that we are soul and feel at one with our physical identity.

We become one with our brain and yet our brain biological memory banks are newly created and hold no memory data. We therefore cannot retrieve memories of whom we are and where we came from as a soul. All that we can experience is to feel within our soul that there perhaps is a bigger spiritual dimension to our lives.

Swamping our senses

The human body presents us with a constant flood of experiences from our very real physical challenges. Our brain manages every aspect of our physical being except our spiritual feelings. Our brain memory areas record our experiences, assimilating some of the information we try to take in and our learning curves. In short, our physical being swamps our senses and almost every moment is focused on our physical activities, our work and education, our relationship, actions and worries. Our spiritual feelings often cannot be made sense of, so we may not prioritize them.

Our brain is our link with the physical world

When a person suffers with Alzheimer's or Dementia the brain sustains damage, often affecting the short-term memory. Subsequently it may change a person's character and make them unable to take care of personal needs. I have given many clairvoyant readings where I connect with a loved one ultimately passed primarily due to such illness. In every single case the person in spirit had given me messages that prove beyond doubt that they are restored to the personality before the onset of brain disease. Usually, their memories are intact but stop at the point in life of the onset of their illness. Loved ones who I am offering the reading to are usually amazed at the contact with their loved one who has the personality and memories from their healthier years. As with every mediumship reading, I have given over many years, the soul in Spirit always retains their memories and their character. This has provided overwhelming evidence that our soul energy retains a full data bank of memories and that our character is truly a reflection of our soul being.

Our brain retains memories, with different areas of the brain for both long and short-term memories. The brain tends to retain more technical information than the soul memory such as telephone numbers.

Recent research has shown an increase in activity of the memory areas of brain when a person is dying. This discovery has been by accident when medical teams were monitoring brain activity for someone seriously ill whom they didn't expect to die. They witnessed much of the brain dying, except the memory areas increased their activity.

The idea of our brain uploading our memories to our soul is not new. Many people who have experienced a drowning incident but were saved describe their "Whole life flashing before them" in almost an instant.

Losing awareness of our soul and the spiritual realm often intensifies people's hurtful behavior. Our brain holds no memories of our spiritual existence before our birth, so it is understandable if people make comments such as "I don't believe in anything spiritual". When people say this to me, I believe they are entitled to their beliefs and make no comment. Their outlook and beliefs are how we are almost programmed to respond by the Higher Creative Power that placed our soul into life as a human being.

The basis of my research has been to discover ideas and concepts that together make sense for people who need logical explanations concerning our spirituality, the existence of Angels and Heaven. The spiritual realm of Heaven is another dimension, so the first logical conclusion is that science will not be able to detect physical evidence of Heaven with scientific instruments. This, and other logical conclusions became a basis of my research.

The second conclusion was that our physical senses are very limited.

The third conclusion was that so-called spiritual experiences that people report should be taken seriously and compared with spiritual experiences reported by other people, perhaps living in other countries and from other cultures.

My research eventually gave me a detailed picture of the meaning of life. It emerged as a picture that made sense and could be explained logically. I had to abandon some, but not all my religious beliefs concerning the human soul and Heaven. As I began to see the universe differently, I began to sense and see the Angels, and I could sense the energies from Heaven. The certainty that I had in understanding the basic meaning of life meant that I could sense Angel energies interacting with all of us and I knew that I could trust those energies with certainty.

So, an important prerequisite to sensing and communicating with the Angels from Heaven is to acquire an understanding that our inner self is a conscious eternal soul whose true home is in the spiritual dimension of conscious energy, Heaven.

An acquaintance of mine is a psychic and medium and was born as a gypsy. In adult life he served in the army and later became an outdoor survival teacher for the army.

At the age of just seven years his parents had him employed in giving readings to the public. The instruction to him was "Just say what comes into your head" To any rational person such an instruction doesn't make sense. However, through my spiritual research listening to what comes into our head can, very cautiously, be taken more seriously. This is because we all have a Guardian Angel who tries to communicate with us.

The learning path towards Intuitive Clairvoyance
The spiritual gifts from learning intuitive clairvoyance do not come overnight. These gifts are acquired gradually over time. Although clairvoyant abilities may come in the order on the above list, they can come in any order. Some people will only acquire modest abilities, others may find their clairvoyance becomes almost miraculous. I teach Foundation Level intuitive clairvoyance, and this knowledge is described in my books. I teach advanced clairvoyance in person only.

*What do we have to do to become
more spiritually intuitive?*

THE BIG SECRET: COMMUNICATE WITH HEAVEN THROUGH OUR INNER THOUGHTS. THOUGHT PROJECTION. The Guardian Angels give us interactive help whenever needed. All that we need to do is overcome the first barrier: satisfying our logical mind with a picture of the System that we can believe

1) Firstly, we need to convince our logical mind that we are spiritual, and that there is an afterlife. This can happen through personal spiritual experience such as a Near Death Experience, or by learning the System I teach and that some or all, of the knowledge fits with your personal beliefs. Many people have a strong inner feeling of their spirituality that conflicts with their logic. I try to present evidence that satisfies the logical mind and allows our inner spiritual feelings to make sense, grow and flourish.
2) Learn the System of the structure of the spiritual dimension. This knowledge cannot be proven by physical science but makes sense logically.
3) Learn about our Guardian Angels as our link with Heaven. Learning how they communicate through our intuitive feelings, conscience, and sudden knowingness.
4) Learn how to be more spiritually intuitive. I only teach intuition that is enabled by our Guardian Angels. This is safe, because we only connect with Heaven, and unconditional love.
5) Learning about negative energies. Negative earthbound energies. Learn about the different types of paranormal phenomena. How to deal with such phenomena. How to protect ourselves from negative energies. Learn how negative energy often builds up to destroy something good. What may take years to build up can be destroyed in seconds or minutes by negative actions or events. This clash of good and evil is the way that earthbound energies seem to work and have always worked.
6) We all have a Life Plan, determined in Heaven before we were born. Learn to discover your Life Plan by being guided

by your Guardian Angel and regain your true path to life fulfilment.
7) Learn about "Energy Vampires". These can be people who control others in a work or close personal relationship. Also, the "Poor Me" people who talk endlessly about their own feelings and drain the emotional and spiritual energies of someone showing care and empathy.
8) Learn about communication in Heaven being enabled by thought projection, and that we can communicate with Heaven by thought projection. A good example of this is prayer.
9) Discover spiritual healing and how Angelic Beings from Heaven bring healing energies to life.

OUTCOMES OF A FOUNDATION IN INTUITIVE CLAIRVOYANCE

Spiritual growth, spiritual strength, and confidence. Less fear of our mortality. Knowing daily guidance from the Guardian Angels to help through life's difficulties. Life fulfilment.

Learning to sense intuition from the Angels helps change our life by changing the way we operate on a deeper level. Rather than just examining our behaviours, habits, and goals, we may delve into our deep-rooted beliefs, our connection to the divine, and discover the real you.

Through the miracle of intuitive clairvoyance, we learn to live by spiritual principles and not the just every-day logic and societal conventions. We may learn how to enable miracles to happen, and help others live happy, fulfilling lives. We can open our inner being to a deepening connection with the non-physical part of ourselves, our soul.

Understanding whom we really are and our world around us from a spiritual perspective can help us lead a more meaningful life. We may discover a profound purpose and that all the events in our life have been orchestrated to bring us to our true path. We can reveal our life purpose and help clear out any energetic blocks to living the life that we were always meant to live. Learning intuitive clairvoyance can help us move into a better, brighter future.

The premise behind most models of spirituality is that we are all here for a reason. Uncovering this reason and living according to our desires is something many people feel leads to true happiness and well-being.

In today's world, we are bombarded daily by messages via the Internet and social media. These messages tend to tell us what we 'should' be doing to be happy and successful. We may be confused and unsure about what it is we really want and need to be happy.

The path to becoming spiritually intuitive will help make these messages fade into the background, allowing ourselves the time and peace we need to connect to our inner voice. This helps us understand what our core desires are and what our true purpose is.

On a personal basis you must establish what is truly important to you. Once you know this, your learning path can be tailored to an action plan to achieve whatever it is that you want. Initially, part of this may include identifying any obstacles that may be holding you back, such as fears, limiting beliefs or old habits. Tapping into your own spiritual power, can help you overcome these.

Another key aspect of sensing Angel intuitive messages is to help you believe in yourself. When you doubt yourself or have low self-esteem, it can be difficult to make progress. This can lead to fear, something that commonly holds people back from achieving their true potential.

A key aim of spiritual intuition is to help you live harmoniously with your life's purpose. This means understanding what your purpose is, eliminating any stumbling blocks you've come up against in the past and realising your inner power. Once this is achieved, amazing things begin to happen.

Tuning in to your inner spirituality

Our Inner Critic

We may not believe we have an "Inner Spirituality" because most of us find that an "Inner Critic" is dominant within us. When we criticise ourselves, reflect on past failures, or believe that we are lacking in motivation, talent, or ability we are listening to our inner critic that seems to stop us moving forward in our life. You might recall a failed exam, a failed attempt to set up a business, a failed job application or a failed personal relationship. Your inner critic tries to make your present and future safe and problem-free so that you don't go through the pain of failure again. Your inner critic distorts and stretches reality so that it only focuses on what you think you can't do. It leaves you feeling lacking in achievement, lacking in fulfilment, and feeling miserable.

Our Inner Coach – our inner connection with our Guardian Angels

Learning clairvoyance starts with helping you discover that you have your own "Inner Coach". Your inner coach speaks from your future reassuring you that everything is going to turn out fine. Yes, you will experience life challenges along the way, but your inner coach sees a great deal more positive and exciting times of happiness, growth, love, and fulfilment.

You may not hear the voice of your inner coach very often because inner critics do a fantastic job of saying you cannot achieve your goals and dreams by reminding you of a grain of truth that convinces you not to move forward with your life towards your dreams of fulfilment.

CHAPTER THREE

Spiritual Development

What is Spiritual Development?

Heaven looks on our Spiritual Development as something that is evidenced by our becoming genuinely more caring and loving to other people, to animals and nature, and to the environment.

We may grow spiritually and develop through life experiences and life challenges to become wiser and to spiritually grow.

What does learning intuitive clairvoyance teach?

1) How we may become closer to our Guardian Angels. They constantly try to help and guide us through our life experiences.

We can develop our spiritual abilities so that we can sense our Guardian Angels with us and learn to recognise how they communicate with us.

What are the benefits of becoming closer in our relationship with Guardian Angels?
- Maximising our spiritual growth.
- Intuitive messages every day guiding us through life to a safer, happier, and fulfilling life.
- Premonitions to help us avoid unwelcome things happening.

Firstly, we need to experience convincing proof of the afterlife and our spiritual nature:

A clairvoyant reading can be a starting point. A healing miracle. NDE's. Witnessing spiritual phenomena. An experience of unconditional love in your life. A premonition. Once we overcome the mental blocks of our logic, we may find ourselves:

1) Becoming aware of the limitations of our physical senses
2) Becoming aware of spiritual energies at the periphery of our perception
3) Learning about thought projection without language. How projecting our thoughts is the way that we communicate in Heaven
4) Learning about Spiritual Healing life energies. Learn about Angels that specialise in healing. Channelling Life energies with the Angels.

Guardian Angels

Angels are real. We all have a Guardian Angel who accompanies us throughout life. We are loved unconditionally by Heaven. We can learn to recognise the way that Angels try help us in many ways as we become spiritually aware of and sense the Angels. The world will become a better place if many more people can learn to be guided by the Heaven in the difficult years of the 21st century that lay ahead.

The teachings concerning Angels in this book are intended to be a foundation in the knowledge needed to sense Angels as a part of the clairvoyant experience. The messages from the Angels and healing that they bring is real, tangible and in many ways miraculous.

Sensing messages from Angels is a form of clairvoyance. However, a naturally gifted clairvoyant and psychic will usually be a person who is more open than most people to sensing spiritual energies. The problem is that they are often open to all spiritual energies, including negative energy and must learn to control how these energies influence them. Messages from Angels can be picked up by learning to open ourselves to the positive energies from Heaven. I call this "Tuning-In to Heaven". The energies from Heaven are always sensed with the unconditional love that Heaven feels for us. Also, we need to learn to recognise negative energies and how to block such energies so they can't influence us.

What form do messages from the Angels take? When a person is advanced with their perceptive abilities they can experience Visions – like video clips or photos in detail and in colour. These are usually accompanied by a sudden "Knowingness" of what the vision means. I see spiritual visions given to me by the Angels when giving people messages, and when experiencing premonitions.

There are many different jobs that Angels do: Guiding, Healing, Guarding, bringing messages and visions, and warnings in the form of premonitions. Our Guardian Angel accompanies us before birth, throughout life, and when passing back to Heaven at the end of our physical life.

Being "Spiritually Open", means having the ability to see, feel and sense spiritual energies. Most people are not born Open because of the danger of being open to negative energies that are so prevalent on the Earth plain. To protect us from negative energies it seems that our memories of Heaven are deliberately blanked off at birth. This also means that most people are not open to the positive spiritual energies from our Guardian Angels that take the form of helpful messages, healing, positive feelings, enhanced intuition, conscience, and love.

We can learn to sense the Angels and recognise the help that they constantly try to give us through messages and healing energies. We might experience a new awareness of Heaven. This can lead us onto a path of enlightenment so that we live our lives with less fear of our mortality, experience physical and mental healing, and greater financial security and life fulfilment. If we learn how to become "In Tune" with our Guardian Angel, we will find a wonderful positive change in our life. We can achieve this more rapidly when we blank our thoughts or meditate for a while.

Learning to blank our thoughts for a few minutes

When we blank our thoughts for just a short while, provided it is safe to do so, we are starting on a path of sensing our Guardian Angel. We live in a time of the most unusual experiences of being human. Many of us work with our brain, our mind, working with a computer screen in front of us. The introduction of smart phones and the emergence of social media leads to many of us occupying every spare moment. We may worry about everything, including relationships, family, health problems, finances, lack of self-fulfilment, career, exams, and all the challenges that life throws at us. We are bombarded by advertising everywhere we turn. We have no spare time in our minds from morning to late evening. Our Guardian Angels cannot be sensed when our minds are busy. No wonder so few people can sense or even believe in Angels.

When I was young, I used to lay awake at night worrying about anything that was currently a problem in my life. I remember lying in bed, unable to sleep, when one night I sensed my Guardian Angel giving me a vision. I could see myself from above. I was looking down at myself with a realisation that "Here I am in bed. It is night-time. What on Earth can I do about my problems right now? What can I achieve lying here, worrying? Isn't it better to get some sleep and then I can tackle my problems tomorrow without being tired?" I then got out of bed, made a note of my problems by writing them down. That cleared my mind. Writing our problems down transfers them out of our thoughts temporarily. The next day, not only did I feel more refreshed, but my problems seemed to be resolved and go away.

Exercise: If you can find a few minutes to stop in your busy life, allow yourself some quiet time. Don't have tv, computers, mobile phones, or radio nearby. Ideally be on your own, in a quiet place. Write down your current problems that might be racing around your brain. Your brain deliberately fires current problems at the forefront of your mind as a survival mechanism. It's as though we are still living a primitive existence and our brain looks on challenges as real physical situations that we need to have in our immediate thoughts. So, when your brain is worrying about finances or anything else, it isn't your inner soul doing this, so write down anything you don't want to forget and allow yourself a few minutes of thinking nothing. It might take some practice. This is the first stage in allowing yourself to become more sensitive to the spiritual energies of your Guardian Angel.

My Personal Spiritual Development

I have been a spiritual researcher for over forty years. My research started following the death of my grandfather. I asked questions to my family and friends about whether we survive physical death. No-one could give me an answer, so I started attending Christian Churches to find out what they believe. I attended the Anglican Church services and study groups, Pentecostal services, Catholic Services, and Methodist services, eventually training as a Methodist preacher. I was baptised with an Anglican Church, a Pentecostal Church, and later confirmed at a Methodist Church. I led over 100 services as a Methodist preacher during a four-year period 2000 to 2004.

Throughout my period as an active Christian, I continued with my spiritual research. My research discoveries led me to a further understanding of Angels, especially our Guardian Angels. I found I could receive messages via the Angels concerning loved ones who have passed. Such messages often include names and other detail that no-one else could know. I learnt how to pass these messages on to people to help them through bereavement grief. I also found that messages were being given to me to help people with worries, fears and problems in life. So, what was happening to me? I began to see our Guardian Angels and receive messages from them. I occasionally had visions of Heaven. These spiritual experiences were accompanied by incredible feelings of unconditional love from Heaven. I was still conducting my spiritual research and, with every experience of our Guardian Angels I would ask questions about the meaning of life. The answers were always given to me, and I began to build up a picture of Heaven.

My belief in God became stronger than ever because of the spiritual experiences. Yet I made my own decision to stand down from training as a Methodist preacher. I did not discuss my spiritual experiences with Christian colleagues because I knew I would be criticised. Visions of Angels and of Heaven are not accepted by many faiths. The basis of Christian learning is Holy Scripture in writings almost 2000 years ago. I will never criticise Holy Scripture because Christian beliefs are still a big part of who I am. People who have strong religious beliefs are best keeping to their faith because it is their strength.

In my logical, questioning mind, through my spiritual research, I have been seeking present day evidence of Heaven, of the Angels and the meaning of life. I felt that with over eight billion people alive on Earth today that there must be evidence surrounding us concerning Angels and Heaven. The media, through television, cinema, and in storytelling produce many dramas and films that present fictional stories about serious crime, horror, war, and the supernatural. Television "Soap Operas" are filled with arguments, crime and people acting in an evil way. All of these give negative spiritual energy too much emphasis in our lives. We need to give emphasis on the miraculous loving power of Heaven and the Angels that try to help us.

The spiritual research that led to me to see and communicate with the Angels gave me a wonderful gift that I want to share with those who are truly interested. This gift works in a way that is equal to the best psychics. The Angels bring messages from loved ones who have passed, including names. They show me the worries and problems around people and communicate helpful messages, guidance, and healing. Angels sometimes give me premonitions of the future.

I am hopeful that at least some of the readers will learn to see the universe differently and gain an increase in spiritual awareness and knowledge of the Angels. Not only is this a wonderful life changing path, but in many ways the ability to sense messages from our Guardian Angels helps to make the world a better place. Heaven has given me permission to teach this knowledge so that the world can face future challenges with many more people living their daily lives, with newly found clairvoyant ability and being guided by Heaven.

A Further Exercise in blanking our Thoughts

The exercise involves clearing away the constant stream of thoughts and worries racing around in our head. To do this we need to blank our thoughts for just a few minutes and tell ourselves that we can recommence our worries afterwards!

One way of blanking thoughts is to sit quietly and bring our attention to the immediate moment, the instant of right now. So, close your eyes and, for just one minute, listen to any sounds in the room, or from outside. After one minute recall the sounds that you heard. If you were doing this right, you would notice that your mind is brought into an awareness of the present moment in time.

The next part of the exercise can be performed in one of two ways. If you have someone in your mind who has passed across to Heaven, think about them but only do this where there was a bond of close friendship or love. If not, just think that you would like to sense your Guardian Angel.

Again, close your eyes and concentrate on the sounds you might hear in the area you are seated. Move your thoughts to this person and say a short prayer to Heaven to give you just one word as a message via your Guardian Angel. You most likely will not hear a word as a voice. The word is usually received intuitively, as if suddenly from nowhere a word has been put into your thoughts. The word might not be identifiable so keep sitting quietly and try to sense intuitively how many syllables in the word, One? Two? Three? What is the first letter or first sound in pronunciation of the word? What do you feel is the actual word? Remember "Just say what comes into your head".

At this point you might feel slightly excited with the experience, or you might feel nothing at all. If so, keep on practising this important exercise. I estimate at this point around 10% of readers will see some success with this. If you feel positive, ask for further words, then sit back and see if the message makes sense. The Guardian Angels will often send words to help you with a current worry or problem in your life.

How do I see Angels?

I do not see Angels all the time. When my soul has been given a vision of Heaven, I have been able to see Angels. I am spiritually grounded and do not see Angels when I am at work or when my mind is occupied by entertainment such as watching tv. At times in life when I have been ill, I have seen them. Angels intensify their energies when they are channelling healing to a person, an animal and to damaged areas of nature and this results in them becoming more visible. I have seen Angels appearing as flashes of light in woodland and I have asked the Angels "What are you doing?". The Angels would reply be telling me that healing energies were being channelled for animals, birds, wildflowers and trees. When I channel healing for a person, I see Angels who are bringing-in healing energies shimmering in different colours depending on the type of healing needed. I see them visibly because they have intensified their healing energies and projected them into the physical dimension.

What do Angels Look Like?

There are many ways that humans describe how Angels appear and what they look like. Angels can appear just as might be expected by the person who experiences a vision of an Angel. In other words, they can change their appearance.

I see Angels without wings, as beautiful male, or female Beings, dressed in robes and radiating light. The light that they radiate, almost as the sun, could be mistaken for wings, especially as visions of Angels often appear suspended in mid-air. They are of another dimension and not affected by gravity.

I am always drawn to the face of an Angel. Their loving eyes tell you that they know everything about you, your good, your bad, and the mistakes you may have made in life. It can be sensed that you are loved unconditionally by Heaven for whom you are.

How do we sense Angels?

For myself, whereas I do not see Angels all the time, I do sense my

Guardian Angel with me all the time. I sense a gentle warmth, and a feeling of being accompanied through life, and a reassurance that Heaven isn't far away.

When I was young, I didn't sense Angels and didn't know what to believe about Heaven. I had much to learn. As experienced by many, many people I went through times when I was lonely, perhaps mildly depressed and feeling cold inside. I believe that learning to sense Angels will help people, so that they have fewer times of feeling cold and lonely.

How do Angels communicate with us?

Angels communicate in many ways. They might give us a sign, a coincidence, or something unusual that we can take as being a message. They communicate through our intuition, our feelings, and our conscience. They might give us intuitive feelings that are warnings to avoid travel or avoid doing something. Angels might communicate with an inner voice, but mostly through an intuitive "Sudden knowingness" in our mind. What they communicate to us will always be positive and will never involve hurting others or hurting ourselves.

I have heard reported unusual happenings which might indicate Angels giving people a sign. One report was of a butterfly that appeared flying around during a funeral service in mid-winter. The lady who told me thought it was a sign concerning her father (whose funeral it was). Other reports are of birds coming close to a person, at the time they were thinking about a loved one who had passed. The bird would not be afraid.

How do we communicate with Angels?

Angels sense our needs and our life problems, so it is not always necessary to communicate with them. When I need special help such as a way forward through overwhelming problems, I make a prayer to the Highest Spiritual Authority in Heaven, to God. The prayer is a form of Thought Projection. The prayer must be made with the purpose of opening a way forward that will not hurt others. Angels work in the purpose of Heaven, and such a prayer, if made with goodness in our heart, is powerful because the Angels act in the purpose of God. Having come from a Christian background I always make a Christian prayer.

Negative Energies

Negative energy is spiritual energy that is the opposite to the energies of Heaven. The energies from Heaven are positive, and creative energies. Negative energies hurt people, hurt nature, and hurt the environment. They are not creative but destructive.

People who hurt others physically or psychologically are working in a negative way. Self-centred people mostly don't care about others because they just think about themselves. A lack of empathy and care indicates a spiritually immature soul. If a person constantly hurt others, then they risk opening themselves up spiritually to negative Earthbound energies. Once negative spiritual energies start to influence a person who lacks empathy then that person will often become worse in their cruel behaviour towards others.

Sometimes people self-harm. This is because they are influenced by negative spiritual energies that want to cause harm. Such a person might say hurtful things to those who care about them. They may also self-harm or behave in an odd way because negative energy seeks to destroy and hurt them.

What is Negative energy?

The human soul has free will to be good or bad in life. Spiritually immature souls are self-centred and more likely to cause hurt. They want money, possessions, and control of others, and are often lacking in empathy. They do not want to understand or care about how others feel at hurt they cause.

Hurting others indicates that a person has a low level of spiritual resonance. When a person behaves in this way then they become almost disconnected from their Guardian Angel. Our Guardian Angel tries to protect us from evil, negative spiritual energies. Once we disconnect from our Guardian Angel then we become spiritually like an open door for the destructive negative energies to influence us.

The influence of negative energies will gradually darken our soul energy. Our soul energy is like a light that surrounds our soul inner core of the "I am". When we pass across to Heaven after physical life, we shed the dark soul energy and it is left behind on the Earth plain. Unfortunately, the dark soul energies that have been left behind by many millions of people is like a reservoir of negative energy, sometimes concentrated in small pockets, and in some ways everywhere. Negative energy is never far away and ready to influence anyone who disconnects from their Guardian Angel because they have been hurting others or nature on a repeated basis.

Having given over six thousand people readings where I passed on messages from the Angels throughout a fifteen-year period, almost everyone I helped found that the messages provided evidence of survival of the soul of a loved one beyond physical death.

At the time of receiving messages, I was invariably overwhelmed by the beauty of the experience and the positive benefit to the person whom I was helping. For me, every time of messages is a time of being close to the Angels and seems like a miracle, as it for most of the people whom I helped. Modern day miracles really can happen. Only afterwards would my enquiring mind think through what had happened. My first thought was usually: "What have I learnt about Heaven from the experience?"

Every time I receive messages, I find the experience to be as different as each of the people I helped. The messages always show me evidence of Heaven from different perspectives, for every person has their own spiritual way of relating to Heaven.

I can understand the religious descriptions of Heaven as being "Holy" with teachings of spiritual love.

The unconditional LOVE in Heaven really is an energy, and that energy is something we need to feel as a part of our natural soul state. We can experience and be a part of that LOVE without religious beliefs.

I can look at Heaven in a mystical way, yet also in a matter-of-fact way, as another dimension that must have its own laws of physics. Above all else the spiritual dimension of Heaven is a place of infinite intelligence. It is the place of what I call "Conscious Energy". Our soul, the real "I" or "Me" inside all of us is made of the same Conscious Energy. Heaven is our familiar, friendly, true home from where we came before birth, and where we return after our physical life as a human being comes to an end.

I know that Heaven wanted me to help people with my gift of seeing and sensing the Angels. Heaven continues to give me visions and messages via the Angels.

When we are receiving messages from Angels we are not speaking to the dead. Communication with Heaven is simply to receive visions and messages from the Angels.

Whenever I do a reading, I realise that I cannot speak with those who have passed. The Guardian Angels from Heaven give me a vision of the person in spirit, and it is the same Angels that give me messages from the deceased soul. Sometimes the person I am giving a reading seeks to ask questions. I must tell them that I find that I cannot ask questions because they will not be answered. Yet, surprisingly the deceased soul, communicating through the Angels would invariably give me messages for the person that were the most important ones. It was as if Heaven knew the questions that were burning inside of the heart of the person I was reading.

Those souls that have been allowed into Heaven, by the Grace of God are not dead to sin, but very much alive in their soul state. The big surprise to myself as I progressed through many thousands of readings to help people who are mostly non-religious, is that most people make it through to a place I name "First Heaven" even if their life was less than perfect. The lives of many people are less than perfect, we all make mistakes in life.

In Heaven, we will all be accompanied by our Guardian Angels to experience a "Life Review" where we be shown the good things we achieved and see the hurt that we have caused others. It is only truly evil people who do not make it to Heaven, usually by their own choice, because they realise that their life review will not be easy. Such evil and tormented souls sometimes choose to stay Earthbound for a while, often manifesting as ghosts or poltergeists. Eventually all these souls are gathered up to be dealt with by Heaven, but not before they have caused some fear and upset as evil earthbound energies.

My training as a Christian preacher did give me the important spiritual gift of "Discernment". This is a true ability to differentiate between good and evil spirits. I can block communication with evil spirits, and only allow the Angels from Heaven to give me messages. I know some clairvoyants who allow any spiritual energy to communicate with them. This can be dangerous, and I believe that this is what Holy Scripture refers to as "It is a sin to speak to the dead". Negative, evil energies do exist in small earthbound pockets, usually attached to a house, historic building, or area of land. They frequently make the most of being able to manifest, causing unnerving physical disturbances using negative spiritual energies.

The overwhelming majority of souls do make it safely to First Heaven, yet once in Heaven then their ability to communicate with those still in life seems almost impossible other than through messages from the Angels. I believe that Heaven respects the right of those in life to live without interference from spirits, good or bad.

TUNING IN TO HEAVEN

As I previously explained this book is not about religion. I am a spiritual researcher and I constantly look for logical explanations before I come to tentative conclusions. My very real spiritual experiences that subsequently came from my spiritual research

have given me personal proof Heaven and the Angels.
Many people use the term "Afterlife" as a general description for a life that our soul will move on to after our physical life ends.

The term "Afterlife" embraces all possible spiritual experiences after we leave our physical life. In my research I have discovered that most souls reach Heaven, even though their lives may have been far from perfect. Perhaps one person in a thousand might choose not to go directly to Heaven because of some traumatic end to their life or because of evil deeds that they committed in life. Negative, evil energy does exist on the earth plane in pockets, whereas Heaven is infinite.
Heaven is another dimension where love is felt as a real, natural energy. It is our familiar true home where we came from before birth. Heaven is a separate place, but it also all around us. We are surrounded in life by spiritual energies that most people are quite blind to. Some of the energies are negative, evil energies which is why we should never open ourselves up to evil. Often, when a person does bad things, such as hurting others, they find it easy to feed off negative energies that seem to boost their ability to continue doing bad things.
I will explain how we can learn to discern between negative energies and the energies of Heaven. By tuning into the Angels and the energies of Heaven we can access the most powerful help. If we learn to tune in to Heaven, the benefits are life changing. We may lose the fear of our mortality. We may begin to access true spiritual guidance and help from Heaven. Those in Heaven whom we call "Guardian Angels" simply try to help us through life. They communicate through our feelings, our intuition, and our conscience. They try to bring healing to us. They can also help us see the future in some significant ways, and more importantly change our futures for the better.
Learning to "Tune-in" to Heaven helps us be closer to our Guardian Angel. With an open mind, determination and love for others and nature we may discover a gradual move forward in life towards Heaven-sent spiritual empowerment beyond our wildest

dreams!

Exercise

When you can find time to sit quietly, then try the following Visualisation:

Close your eyes and imagine yourself in a dark room. The room has no windows, and the door is closed. There is no light, and you realise that all Is completely black. You are feeling as if you are floating in a dark void.

Now imagine the door slightly open. An intense, beautiful light shines through the opening and starts to drive away the darkness. The door opens further, and the beautiful light now fills the room. Outside all you can see is Light.

Now, feel yourself moving out of the door outside into the Light. There is nothing to see only Light surrounding you. You are relaxed and sense a gentle warmth. The energy you notice and start to feel is that of unconditional love within the Light and surrounding you.

Keep drifting forward in the Light, and before you visualise a garden full of flowers, radiating every colour. Feel yourself drawn into the garden and visualise the beauty of the flowers surrounding you.

At the head of the garden, visualise an Angel. Flowing robes of white, radiating and shimmering with energy. Find yourself drawn to the face of the Angel and look at the eyes of the Angel, looking at you with unconditional love. You realise that you are loved for whom you are, all the good, and all the mistakes.

In your visualisation stay in this garden with your Guardian Angel for as long as you wish. When you are ready, pull out of the visualisation, open your eyes and just sit relaxing for a few minutes.

You might need to read through the visualisation several times before you try it. Alternatively, you could ask someone who you know is interested to narrate the visualisation gently and slowly.

Summary of the Exercise

Yes, you have just used your imagination for this exercise. However, the visualisation is a real example of entering the Light of Heaven. It is a building block in opening-up your spiritual awareness of Angels. Success rate in this exercise averages 50%. Unsuccessful averages 25% of people honestly saying that they are incapable of visualising, and the final 25% saying that visualising was easy, but they didn't feel anything spiritually.

See the Universe Differently

During the early years of my research, I made an amateur study of Quantum Mechanics, and was fascinated by the theories of parallel universes, and observations that the tiniest particles of matter appeared to behave in strange ways. At sub-atomic level, the tiniest particles of matter can appear from nowhere and disappear into seemingly nowhere.

I began to visualise solid objects around me in a different way. Everything is made of unimaginable vast amounts of energy within the atoms. Invisible energy that holds things together. I could look at a wooden table, and then visualise it as semi-transparent with nothing in between the atoms and molecules except invisible energy.

I thought about radio and television signals travelling through the air at the speed of light, carrying vast amount of information, yet we see and feel nothing unless we have equipment that can convert these signals back into video and audio.

I read that Quantum Mechanics has a theory that is named "The Spooky Theory". An electron can cause another electron at the other side of the universe to instantly move in the same way at the same time. We make use of the Spooky Theory when speaking on the phone, when using apps, and when using any computerised device. Have you ever questioned how messaging, or use of apps is an instantaneous process? Most people just accept these things without asking questions.

All these observations show us that our physical senses are quite limited. Our eyes pick-up light, our ears pick-up sound. Then we have the senses of smell, taste and touch, and that's it!

I began to realise that we can't see, hear, touch, smell or taste spiritual energies that are very real.

Who or what are we?

Our soul energy is made of the same stuff that I call "Conscious Energy" that populates Spiritual Realm of "Heaven". This is nothing spooky or weird, and nothing to be frightened about because Heaven is our true home.

An important gift when learning to sense Angels is the gift of Discernment between good spiritual energies, and negative, evil spiritual energies. Sometimes evil can often show itself as good so the ability to truly discern is an acquired skill that must be gradually developed.

There are spiritual energies around us all the time, mainly from the Angels, helping, guiding, and constantly trying to heal and sustain life, including ourselves.

Spiritual energies sustain life and are simply named as "Life Energies". I believe that Life Energies are programmed – like a computer operating system. Our body is the "Hardware", and our everyday tasks are the "Application Software" or "Apps". Life Energies keep our body working and bring-in healing.

In our everyday experience as human beings we may not notice the faint spiritual energies at the outer edge of our perception.

With enhanced knowledge of Heaven, and the Angels we can look out for these energies and learn the first steps in recognising them.

There is an almost impenetrable barrier between the Spiritual Realm, and the physical universe in which we are temporarily in life dwelling. I say "Almost" because there are energies there that we can, with the correct knowledge, recognise, interpret, and respond to.

Much of the spiritual activity that can be sensed is from the Angels, especially our own Guardian Angels.

Sensing Angels: Many people Question "Are We Spiritual?"

The most basic questions are all connected: Are we spiritual? Is there a Heaven? Is there any form of spiritual afterlife?

Science tells us that we do not have a soul and that a Heaven cannot exist because science is unable to find evidence that these exist. The most common ways that human beings can accept that there is a spiritual dimension and that we ourselves have a soul are through either religious beliefs or personal spiritual experiences. In modern times so called "Near Death Experiences" have become widely recorded. This is because many people who have been near death due to injury or serious illness have been saved by modern day professional medical help. During their time at the closest point to death some estimates indicate that around 17% of people experience an out-of-body spiritual event that can be recalled later. These NDE experiences can be totally convincing and life changing. Sometimes those experiencing an NDE can recall seeing their Guardian Angel.

The following is an account of a NDE based on a true experience: Peter was proud of his motor bike and travelled everywhere on it, including travel to work. Kate, his girlfriend constantly worried about him riding his bike because he seemed oblivious to danger, especially in bad weather situations. The day that he had his accident was a weekend and he decided to visit his parents who lived nine miles away from his home. The weather was quite bad with heavy rain and strong winds as he travelled on a country road out of town. His bike suddenly hit a bump in the road that knocked his steering. The bike started to swerve uncontrollably on the wet road surface. He came off the road and hit a tree and everything went black.

Peter found himself awake in hospital. He was looking down at a hospital bed with a doctor and two nurses attending someone who was unconscious. It took him a moment to realise that the person they were attending was himself. He didn't feel concerned, nor did he feel afraid. He felt good and yet he knew what the doctor and nurses were thinking. The nurses were thinking "He won't make it. He is going to die". The doctor was thinking "I will try my best to save him".

Peter found himself being drawn to a light at the side of the room. The light seemed warm and inviting as he entered its loving embrace. He was moving at high speed in what seemed like a tunnel at the end of which was the source of the light. He could see the vague outline of two people stood in the light. Suddenly he found himself in a calm, beautiful meadow. The grass was green, and flowers of every shade seemed to shine with a vivid intensity that left him lost for words. Peter was surprised at how he felt. All his senses were working yet he had no physical body. His soul energy was his body. He felt as though this was the true reality of home. Unconditional love was around him like the air that he had breathed in life. Peter also experienced a profound feeling of oneness with the universe.

He was met by his grandma who he knew had died last year. His grandad was stood with her. He had died nine years earlier. "It is not your time," said his grandma. Peter felt totally unconcerned about the life he had just left. "Can I stay here?" said Peter. His grandma did not reply as a spiritual being appeared in the form of person but radiating light and he felt that this was an Angel. The Angel had no wings and appeared with white and purple radiant garments and a presence that felt loving but strict, with some spiritual authority. "You have things to do that we planned for you in your life. You must go back", said the Angel. "Are you, my Guardian Angel?" asked Peter. Before he received a response, he suddenly felt himself much heavier and began to feel some discomfort and pain. He opened his eyes and realised that he was back in his body in a hospital bed. A nurse saw that he had regained consciousness and he heard her say to a colleague "He is awake, thank goodness, I thought we had lost him".

Peter eventually made a full recovery although he never rode a motor bike again. He was reluctant to tell people about his NDE, but he did tell his girlfriend Kate. Kate was the person who told me about this when she came to me for Angel messages. During the consultation I was given a message that her boyfriend had been injured in a motor incident and that it had changed his life. She confirmed to me that Peter had experienced this life changing event and that it had made him more caring towards her and others. Peter was no longer scared at the thought of death, but now knew that it was only the beginning of another stage in the eternal life of his true inner being.

The following is a further true account of an NDE, but a different experience:

Alison was on holiday with her sister at a popular seaside holiday resort on the south coast of England. The weather was hot and sunny, so they headed for the beach. There were lifeguard stations so the two felt totally at ease as they walked into the sea. "I'll race you swimming up to that buoy" said her sister Carol. The buoy floated bright orange about two hundred yards off the beach. It was probably something securing a fishing pot for catching lobsters or crabs. Alison reached the buoy first and turned to see Carol approaching her and looking frustrated because she came second. The girls, both aged in their twenties, held position together at the buoy. "The water is cold!" shouted Alison. "Come on let's get back to the beach and warm up in the sun". "You go first" she said to Carol. "I will still try to win".

Carol lunged forward to swim towards the beach in the cold sea water. Alison waited a few seconds then struck forward to swim back. Suddenly her arms and legs went into severe cramp. The shock of the cold sea was hitting her. She struggled to keep swimming but the harder she tried the more her arms and legs screamed with pain. She could no longer swim and found herself being submerged. She tried to get her head above water and screamed for help. The cold sea started to swallow her. It seemed quite deep and small waves that she hadn't really noticed were hindering her attempts to gasp a mouthful of air. She realised she was drowning and going under. Her senses of panic overwhelmed her. In her mind her life flashed before her. Every minute of her life could be vividly seen, ending in her sadness at the memory of her daughter, now aged two years, at home with her partner Mike who was at home while she took a day out with her sister.

The pain in her limbs disappeared and then she felt herself in a place of blackness. She couldn't understand what has happened to her but didn't feel frightened. A small light appeared in the distance, racing towards her and getting bigger as it approached. The light quickly reached her, and she felt at ease and surrounded by light. The light enveloped like a warm blanket of love as she saw in the light an Angel and her father who had died the previous year. The Angel looked on with love as her father gave her a message: "It's not your time Alison. Tell your mother I love her and that I still watch over her". Another beautiful Angel then came into view. Without words she knew it was her Guardian Angel who knew everything about her, her good and bad, and loved her unconditionally for whom she was and is.

The moment on the edge of Heaven came to and ended as she awoke coughing up sea water, gasping for breath. She felt cold like she had never been before, and her breathing was painful. She was alive. The lifeguards had been quick to act when they heard her screams before she went under the water. Carol was with her and held her hand as she was taken by stretcher into an ambulance and then on to the local A&E hospital.

After an overnight stay in hospital Alison made a full recovery.

Many months later she came to see me for Angel messages. Her father came through and her Guardian Angel brought through a vision of this incident that Alison confirmed as correct. Her life had been changed forever by her near-death experience and she felt spiritually stronger. Alison was happy and deeply moved emotionally to hear messages from her father.

As with most people who have experienced an NDE she now seemed to value every moment of every day as a blessing and life as a precious gift. Her experience of life flashing before her eyes as she was drowning has led to questions in my spiritual research.

This is quite a common experience.

Question to Heaven: "Why do some people see their life flashing before them at the time of near death?

Message from Heaven: "The human brain has a memory and so does the spiritual soul of a person. At the time of near death, the brain is programmed to upload as much memory as possible to the soul. The memory bank of life experiences is important to the soul as the person transitions back from physical life to Heaven. The brain is one of the first organs to die. Again, this is by deliberate design so that the soul of a person can be released quickly when life in the physical body is at an end.

My preferred description of our soul is "Conscious Energy". Our soul is made of this energy and the spiritual dimension is that of Conscious Energy.

The main spiritual dimension of what we may describe as "Heaven" is one where the energy of love is at its greatest natural state. Love can be just an emotion but in its purest form Love is an energy. The dimension of Heaven is almost infinite. The opposite to love is negative energy, or in its worst form it is described as evil. Negative energy is earthbound and exists in small, localised pockets.

CHAPTER FOUR

How Angels interact with us

Angels sometimes give us visions through our Third Eye
When learning to sense Angels it is beneficial to learn how to interpret images that come into our mind. Are such images generated from our inner memories, or, if images are unexpected, are they spiritual?
The Third Eye is not a physical eye, it is our spiritual eye.
When we see images in our mind then these can be memories that have been stored by our brain and re-created as images.
If I said to you "Visualise a pace where you went on holiday", then you might see an image of that place in your mind's eye. The image would have been retrieved from the memory in your brain and brought instantly to the front of your mind.

Such images can also be held in our soul memory. I know this because every time the Angels bring messages from a loved one who has passed, they also give me images of almost anything they wish to communicate. These images are still held in the soul memory of the person now in Heaven, having been retained whilst they were in life.

If we allow ourselves to stop occasionally and blank our thoughts through mediation, then we might allow our third eye to pick up random images.

This is a spiritual time we might allow ourselves to not recall a holiday or anything else because we are deliberately not allowing ourselves to think about the past, present or future.

Of course, random images might not appear in our mind. After all, why should any image appear when we have quietened our thoughts?

I always blank my mind of thoughts before I connect with the Angels to bring messages for someone. I clear my own thoughts completely and leave myself open to whatever my Angel Guide places in my mind. It could be an image of a deceased person who has a love connection with the person I am with, or a place, or an item of clothing, or anything. I would also, at the same time, receive messages that accompany the image as a sudden "Knowingness"

I will give some examples of how images might be given to me in my Third Eye:

If I am giving a reading, it is usually to connect with a loved-one who has passed. I would be given images by my Angel Guide, who will be working with the Guardian Angel of the person sat in front of me, and the Guardian Angel of the person in Heaven. The first image I am usually shown is the image of the person who has passed. Often, they appear at the side of the person I am reading. I am free to scan up and down the vision of the deceased person. I will usually start by describing whether I am seeing a male or female, old or young, with an approximate age. I can see their hairstyle, hair colour, and their face. I would see if they wore much make-up, and describe dress jewels such as a ring, or necklace.

I am often drawn to what they are wearing, and the colour and style of their clothing. Sometimes this can be comical, and the humour will be from the person in spirit who might admit to having worn the same slippers for many years, hence they seem well worn. I have had men in spirit deliberately show me an image of holes in their socks. This would have been true to life, and a genuine attempt by a person in spirit to reassure that the Heaven is not without laughter, but a place where we can retain a sense of humour. Indeed, the clairvoyant readings consistently show that we retain our character in the Heaven. This is because we are all unique, and our character is not just our brain, but our inner, eternal soul that we call "Me" or "I".

Current Life Help from Angels

When I receive Angel messages concerning the current life problems and difficulties of someone, then the person in front of me doesn't want to connect with a loved one who has passed. He or she is wanting to know if I can see what is happening in their life, and what can I tell them concerning their future. Again, my Angel Guide works with their Guardian Angel to give me messages that are relevant. I would see these as images that mean nothing to me, but when I describe what I see are of importance to the person in front of me. I am also given knowledge as a "Sudden Knowingness", and I hear words, especially names. I describe what I see and hear, and the messages from the Angels will progress from there.

When I say "Progress", I mean that I start to see images of their future, and I receive messages concerning their future.

When a person has told me nothing, except to confirm what I say, they are usually amazed about things I describe concerning their past and present life. However, I often tell them "Look, you have come to see me because you want to know what the future holds. Yes, I give thanks when the Angels give me messages about your past and present when I knew nothing about you, but you already know your past and present, so it is only worth seeing me if the Angels are willing to tell you about your future".

Sensing the Future

It seems amazing when a person with Psychic gifts gives a Fortune Telling Reading. We might think to ourselves "How do they do it".

In my spiritual research I question "How do such amazing thoughts come into the mind of a psychic?"

The answer is, of course, that someone is helping them. Most psychics would readily agree that it is their Spirit Guide who helps them. I only ever connect spiritually with Angels, especially our Guardian Angels.

Our Guardian Angels know our Life Plan. Yes, we all have a Life Plan determined in Heaven before we were born, and our Guardian Angels know our Life Plan, and know some of our future.

Our own Free Will is commonly understood to have led us to where we are today and defines our actions and future Life Events. My research has surprisingly led to the conclusion that future events on our Life Plan will happen irrespective of our daily free will decisions.

However, some people live lives without empathy and disconnect from sensing their Guardian Angel. Their future life could be way off course from that planned in Heaven. These are the people who cause damage and destruction on our planet.

Free will influences our daily routine yet, we can sacrifice some of our free will to another person when in a close relationship with them. We can sacrifice some of our free will by caring for someone and helping them in everyday tasks.

The Future is linked to the Past

The key discovery in my learning about how the Angels see the future was when I came to the realisation that much of the future is determined and planned in the past. What has been planned for us is then steered by our Guardian Angel into happening in immensely powerful spiritual ways to become our future reality.

However, this process is frequently prevented by our individual spiritual free will. If we don't understand, if we can't or don't want to listen to Heaven, then the good positive things planned for our personal future might not happen. Life then becomes a struggle that can last for many years, or even a lifetime.

The heading "Aspects of the Soul" explains in detail how we might receive guidance from Heaven, through our Guardian Angels trying to help and guide us.

How was our future life planned? This process is simply determining a "Life Plan". Our Life Plan seeks to remedy things that we need to correct, and to give us the opportunity to learn to enable our further spiritual development.

Past Lives

Most of us will have experienced life as another person prior to our present life. We may have had many lives. The person that we truly are inside, the "I" or "Me" has been shaped by previous lives. This "Shaping" contributes to our character and our driving forces in this life.

Firstly, it is essential that we identify our Driving Forces. We can ask ourselves questions such as: "Am I adventurous or shy? Am I outgoing or not? Do I enjoy challenges or not? Am I outspoken?"

Secondly, we need to accept that we have a Life Plan, which was determined before we were born. We all have a Life Plan that our Guardian Angels know. We need to identify our Life Challenges that were included in the Life Plan.

What was planned for our future can often be perceived by taking seriously the inner visions of who we always wanted to be, and our inner thoughts of what we always wanted to do.

CHAPTER FIVE

ASPECTS OF THE SOUL

Our Behaviour in Life is governed by the Aspect in which our soul resonates.

When we try to determine why people behave as they do, we have the medical science of psychology.

When we try to determine a person's behaviour spiritually, we can identify that behaviour is frequently linked to our relationship with our own Guardian Angel. This relationship is governed by three major aspects to our soul:

Our Higher Self
Our Middle Self
Our Lower Self

Middle Self
I have started to explain Middle Self first because most people live in this Aspect most of the time. The Middle Self is the Centre of our Aspect Being. We may describe this as self-centred behaviour. We have to be self-centred to survive in life. This means making sure

we have enough food, clothing, somewhere to live, money.

In modern, materialistic society our souls are constantly groomed into resonating with the Aspect of the Middle Self. Advertising is everywhere we turn, internet, radio, tv, newspapers and magazines. Our physical brain brings sensations through sight, sound, smell, taste, touch, and desire for positive physical experiences and adventures. Our soul resonates in what we think is a "Normal" way with Middle Self. We are swamped with advertising messages of how we can acquire the material things we desire.

The modern materialistic world is not the normal human experience if we go back in the past to see how human beings lived in simpler times.

The human soul is groomed by society into choosing the Middle Self Aspect. This is our Free Will choice, that our Guardian Angels must respect, yet it means that our we, our soul, may not resonate in the Higher Self as often as we should.

Lower Self
There are several Spiritual Aspects within the Lower Self. Our Lower Self is primitive, aggressive, survival self:

Many people living in their Lower Self Aspect may have very little conscience. They are capable of hurting people psychologically, and physically. They don't often feel compassion and will cause suffering with no ability to "Put themselves in others' shoes to see how others feel". They enjoy controlling others, especially people who are in a close relationship with them. They drain the energy of people close who are trying constantly to please them.

Another Aspect of Lower Self can be seen in people who constantly feel self-pity. The "Poor Me" syndrome. These people have one thing in common with those previously described in (1) in that they drain the energy of people who are close to them.

An important aspect of Lower Self is where society influences people deliberately to resonate part of their time in their Lower Self. One example is that of soldiers in wartime situations. They are groomed by their training to resonate in the aggressive survival self, yet in their personal lives would move back their Soul Aspect to resonate in their "Normal" Middle Self, and sometimes in their Higher Self. Guardian Angels may, or may not, still be close to people in these situations. The reasons become extremely complex.

Living in our Lower Self Aspect, if it is by our own Free Will choice, leaves us left cut-off from our Guardian Angels. We may live a life in stress, and constant anger, or depression. We may gain physical advantages over others for a time and acquire short term success over others. We also are at high risk of negative energies taking over our soul.

Higher Self
When we live in the Aspect of our Higher Self, we are show love and compassion for others, and for animals and nature. We might put the interests of others ahead of ourselves.

The absolute Attribute to resonating in the Higher Self is to be able to feel and project Unconditional Love. We will then be "In Tune" with Heaven.

I personally, live and resonate within my Middle Self most of the time. It keeps me grounded, and functioning in the real world and society we live in. When I need to help someone spiritually, I connect to my Higher Self by firstly moving my thoughts to feel and project unconditional love. This moves myself into the Higher Self Aspect of closeness with my Guardian Angel, and I receive visions and messages.

Most people can move themselves for short periods into the Higher Self. If you see a baby, or a kitten or puppy, you will notice how you may feel unconditional love… and this is an intense feeling that momentarily might leave you feeling "Better" because you started to resonate in your Higher Self.

Our soul needs to be capable or resonating in our Higher Self to be an Intuitive Clairvoyant.

When we are resonating in our Higher Soul Self we will feel the unconditional love from Heaven as a real, powerful energy. When we help others using our spiritual gifts, we must be a channel of the unconditional love from Heaven. Spiritual healing energies travel on the energy pathway of unconditional love. Such love can be compared to a spiritual road on which such energies flow.

Guardian Angels connect with our Higher Self
We all have Free Will to choose whether we live in the aspect of our Higher Self or choose to dwell in our Middle or Lower Self Aspects.

However, we can only know a true connection with our Guardian Angels when we choose to live in the Aspect of our Higher Self.

Our Guardian Angel is the BRIDGE between Heaven - of Unconditional Love- and the physical world in which we live. The Healing energies and wisdom of the Heaven are made available to us via our Guardian Angels.

How we may learn to Live more in the aspect of our Higher Self
Our soul energy shimmers and resonates at different levels, moving and changing within the different Aspect Levels many times each day. We may exist mainly in the Middle Self, mainly in the Lower Self, or mainly in our Higher Self Aspect.

Human beings can resonate Higher Self by focussing on the spiritual energy of unconditional love. We can achieve this in many ways: by helping and caring for others, through prayer, through building-up rather than breaking down (Have you ever noticed that a house can take months to build, a relationship can take years to build...that is how good and positive things are done. Negative energy can destroy a building, destroy a relationship in seconds).

As we start to spiritually grow, by our own Free Will, to resonate more often in the Aspect of our Higher Self, our Guardians will naturally be closer to us, and we will FEEL their closeness

1) We will not feel that cold, insecure feeling inside, but instead a gentle warmth of love, of inner confidence and spiritual strength

2) When we are helping others, or doing something good and positive, we will find a new energy to get through the work we need to do. This energy is channelled from our Guardian Angel and is especially noticeable when we are otherwise tired. When we help others or help animals, nature or the environment we will be resonating in Higher Self if our soul is truly loving and caring. This state of Higher Self is also a state of being In Tune with Heaven and brings associated gifts of healing and seeing some of the future. Charity work or any kind of help we offer brings healing to a situation where there is suffering. Also, the ability to see the future if no help was given, and the ability to change the future for the better if help is given.

3) Our Guardian Angels works through our feelings to bring healing and calm into situations

4) In some people who are dedicated to truly helping others their Guardian Angel works so closely with the Higher Self, that their energies meld to the point where that person is almost an Angel

5) Living in the Aspect of our Higher Self we may no longer feel depressed

6) Living in the Aspect of our Higher Self means that we can experience our Guardians giving us messages through our FEELINGS, INTUITION, and CONSCIENCE

7) Our Guardian Angels know our Life Plan. We may be given "Insights" into our future Life Plan through pictures in our soul-mind

8) In our Higher Self Aspect, we can keep tunnel vision in what we really want in our future, and our Guardian Angels will put things in place to make our dreams come true, other than winning money!

CHAPTER SIX

Angels at work

The Angels try to speak to us through our intuition, which is the starting point of how they communicate. When I give people a reading, people in my audience often comment that they sense a calm, healing atmosphere. My Angel Guide shows me a vision of those who are spiritually very much alive in Heaven and will pass on messages from loved ones. I am shown images of places and objects that may mean something to the person I am reading. I may also see what has happened, and what is happening in the lives of those whom I read and ask my Angel to show me the Life Path for that individual, to help them back on the correct path to fulfilment and happiness.

Angels help in the following ways: Angels speak to us through our intuition. Have you ever struggled with a problem, unable to find an answer, then suddenly the answer is there? Have you ever been overwhelmed by stress and worry, and then somehow you work through the situation? Have you ever had a gut feeling that you shouldn't go somewhere, and later discover that you are glad you listened to your intuition? …. or maybe you didn't listen to your intuition and regretted doing something? Your Guardian Angel helps you through your intuition. There is no language, just an instant awareness of what we should or shouldn't do by a form of telepathy which we don't acknowledge because we don't realise that we are being helped. In some people the fine tuning of their intuition can lead to an individual becoming in some ways clairvoyant. If we pray to God for healing, then a Healing Angel will help bring healing directly to the person suffering, both spiritually, and through those working to help medically.

Angels can be with us to give us STRENGTH. Both physical, and emotional strength.

A Prayer to God is essential. Angels can be with us to guide us through life's problems and difficulties.

Angels helping us in our daily lives can only be appreciated if we believe in God and the Angels.

A word of caution: Angels rarely communicate as a voice in your head unless to give a sudden warning of imminent danger. A voice in your head is not allowed because a voice telling us what to do would go against our "Free Will" to live our lives as we choose. Also, an Angel of God would never be a nuisance by bothering you in ways you don't want. Angels of God certainly never guide us with bad thoughts.

How can a belief in Angels help you?

If you can find somewhere quiet where you can spend a few minutes on your own. It could be just another room in your home. Sit quietly, relax, and try, just try to blank your mind and think of nothing for just one minute. What can you achieve by worrying about the past or future? So, sit quietly and try to appreciate the intensity of the moment of "Now". Listen to any background sounds even in the quietness. Did you succeed? Remember, just no thoughts for one minute. In Heaven, time does not exist. There is only the "Now". Time is purely a physical thing…. the revolution of the Earth, the hours in the day, the days in a year. We should learn to live more in the moment of the "Now" and appreciate every moment of your life as a gift from God…………… even in the hardest of times.

Right, now as you sit quietly think about your most pressing problem at the moment. Quietly say a prayer to God, or think a prayer in your mind, and ask for help. Then, leave it at that……………you have passed your problem up to God. Within minutes, hours, or a day or so you may be surprised how suddenly you become aware of an answer to your problem. Alternatively, you may just feel better about yourself, and the problem will be something that you find the strength and wisdom to handle.

This "Sudden answer" is real help from your Guardian Angel. So how has the Angel communicated? Well, by helping you, the feeling of being helped, the intuition that you receive. Sensing Angels gives you greater certainty that there is life after death. This helps you personally handle grief from bereavement better. You can never get over bereavement, yet you can get through it. It helps you see that your own life is just part of an eternal process of the life of your soul. Your soul is the bit inside of you that you know as "I" or "Me". Messages from Angels can help people with problems in their lives including problems of finances, relationships, stress, ill health, worry, insecurity, lacking in fulfilment. Angels can see situations surrounding people. Giving them messages that are of real help often astonishes people and helps them believe. This opens minds to show them that they can receive spiritual love, strength, wisdom and support. It is even possible to look at their future life-plan to get them back on course

As a person who can receive messages from the Angels, I find it easy to see some things in the future for a person that I am giving a reading. However, while these things I see are always good, positive things that a person would want, I realise that the same person might still be going through life difficulties, things going wrong in their life that seem terribly unfair.

When I see a person's future, images appear in my mind's eye. The mind's eye can also be called the "Third Eye". The images appear in a way that is familiar to all of us. For example, if I say "Visualise "Big Ben in London", even though you might have never been there, you will have seen photos or video of Big Ben, and an image might appear in your mind.

I am often given images of the future of things that are not familiar to me, but absolutely relate to the person I am reading. It could be a new home, a new car, or an image of a person whom they are yet to meet in a new friendship. It could be a place they might travel, a new job, or success in sport, or artistic achievement.

The images come into my mind easily as visions, but fortune tellers might use visual aids such as cards, a crystal ball, or even reading tea leaves!

Spiritual Energies in Nature

When out walking I often see flashes of light, especially in woodland and near streams, rivers and lakes. The Angels are constantly trying to maintain nature, and I see their light energies as they intensify when bring in healing to trees, plants, animals and birds. I can understand why folklore legends of fairies and other mythical creatures exist as some people may have seen the same flashes of light.

Spiritual Energy controls nature. Migrating birds "Know" where to go as they travel many thousands of miles because intelligent spiritual energies guide them. Homing pigeons are guided in the same way. Scientists believe that these birds are guided by the magnetic field, as used in a simple compass. The Earth's magnetic field only work North to South, not fully 360 degrees as would be necessary to use it for guidance.

CASE STUDIES
A reading, where an Angel brings messages from a loved one who has passed, can change a person's future

INTUITIVE CLAIRVOYANCE

I gave Angel messages to a lady called Anne. I had never met her before, and she appeared to be aged in her early seventies. The only question I asked is for her name, and then I asked her to say nothing, except to confirm or otherwise the things I would describe.

I immediately given a vision of a lady in spirit whom I knew to be her mother. She was stood, as they usually do, to the left side of Anne. I described her mother's hair. It was grey, not coloured, and curly. This is where I am not very good at description because I don't know the names of different hairstyles. I told Anne my vision and I said, "It looks like her hair was nicely kept, and "Permed". Anne smiled for the first time and confirmed what I was seeing. "She is wearing a dark blue cardigan and black skirt". "That will be her, she often dressed exactly like that," said Anne.

Then my Angel suddenly gave me the name "Dorothy" spoken into my mind. "I have the name Dorothy" I said. Anne confirmed: "Yes, that was my mother's name".

My Angel Guide then gave me a vision in my Third Eye of her mother in bed, very sick, with Anne caring for her. I heard the words "Please thank her". I relayed the message to Anne that she had to care for her mother. I knew instantly that this had meant that Anne had to live with her mother towards the end of her mother's life. I said to Anne "I can see that you sacrificed a lot to live with your mother to care for her. She thanks you for that". Anne began to show emotional tears and was overwhelmed in a happy way to receive the message of thanks. I then saw a vision of a locket, holding a photo of her mother. I described the locket to Anne, and she pulled it out from where it was hidden behind her coat. It was exactly as described. I went on to give more detail that her mother communicated to me.

At the end of the reading Anne told me how she had previously held no beliefs in a life after death. She had felt insecure and cold inside following the recent death of her mother. Her life, her future, was changed for the better. She knew absolutely that no-one could have given her the information that came through the

61

reading. She knew it was her mother. She would no longer carry the heavy weight of grief. She could move forward with her life feeling better.

Here is a case where a lady age around thirty years was able to see a brighter future following help from the Angels

Leanne came to see me. She seemed quite happy and bright. When I give a reading my first thought is "Do they want Angel messages from a love-one who has passed, or do they want messages concerning their life issues?" I never ask them this question. My Angel Guide usually points me in the right direction quite rapidly. In this case it was a need for guidance concerning life issues. I saw that she was no longer in a relationship with a partner, and that she had two young children. As I began to tell her, Leanne confirmed that as correct. Suddenly I saw a vision of her being mentally and physically abused and attacked by her ex-partner, and that this had happened on a regular basis. This was quite a dramatic vision, and as I relayed and described this to her, she confirmed that this was exactly how her relationship had been. She had escaped her relationship in fear of her life.

"It isn't over yet" is what I told her. "Your ex-partner is still making threats to personally harm you". That is correct" she said. "I have a Court Injunction that states he cannot come near my house, but he is so violent that it sometimes doesn't stop him trying to get to me. I need to move home, live somewhere that he can't find me"

I then realised that the Angels were giving me visions of the future for her. I saw a new man in her life. A very caring person. I described him in detail starting with his hairstyle and hair colour, the shape of his face, his stature, and the clothes he might typically wear. Leanne had a look of amazement as she opened-up a photo on her phone. "Is this him?" she asked. The photo was exactly the image I could see in my vision. She was astonished at my description of this new man and felt she might start to trust this new relationship that she had found. I then told her that he had been in a relationship that had failed, and that he had one child, a daughter, with shared custody with his ex. She confirmed this.

I concluded by describing a vision of her spending her future life with him, much happier, and able to move away from her current location. I gave her a warning that this new man could be prone to being quiet and moody after finishing work, and that he is quite serious in his work as a baker. Leanne laughed and said that she could cope with that.

At the end, she expressed amazement at how I could have known the information that I had given her. She felt that her fear and reluctance to move on with her life could now be worked through, and that she could gradually, step by step, move forward in her new relationship.

Sensing Angels

Learning how to sense Angels is important. It is achieved as part of our personal spiritual development. We don't need to sense Angels all the time.

I can't sense Angels when I am at work or watching television or doing anything that occupies my mind. In the 21st century most of us are occupying our minds with work, entertainment, social media, and countless other thoughts. Many people stay awake at night worrying about things. The Angels can only be sensed when our mind is quiet. In order to sense Angels for yourself the first thing to do is allow yourself some quiet time. You do not necessarily need to spend time in a quiet room. You could be out walking on a safe, quiet path, away from traffic.

Angels are from Heaven, but if we try too hard to sense spiritual energies, we might feel uncomfortable because we might also sense negative energies.

We need to say a prayer, in our mind to the God, or the Highest loving Source in whom you believe. Pray for the ability to sense Angels from Heaven. Prayers can be heard because in Heaven we speak to each other using our thoughts. It is important to pray for protection from evil, negative energies. In our prayers ask to be guided by Heaven, given strength by Heaven, and be totally protected from negative energies that might seek to hurt ourselves or our families.

We should try to sense Angels in different settings. In a quiet room can you sense a gently, loving someone with you?
Whilst out walking in woodland can you sense the unseen spiritual energy of the trees as if they are looked after by an Angel? I have witnessed Angels in woodland settings, especially near a stream, as flashes of light. This happens when they bring healing to nature and the healing energies of the Angels intensify. Often, when I see these flashes of light, I think that such visions could account for people witnessing fairies and other mythical creatures. Of course, I always ask questions when I see an Angel, and the usual explanation when I see them in nature is to be shown the tree, flower, or plant that the Angels is healing. This can also be a rabbit, bird, or other wildlife. Often the healing is for an entire area of forest or vegetation.
Many people feel a sense of exhilaration and well-being when walking in the countryside. At times we may experience a scenic view and our spiritual senses seem heightened in awareness. With an understanding of Angels who are close to us, but often unseen, we can sense them intensely when we are experiencing heightened spiritual awareness.

Observing People.
Without making it obvious that you are looking at people, it is interesting if you sit on a park bench and glance at people walking by. You might be surprised at the sudden knowingness that comes into your mind concerning people. You might sense them feeling stressed, happy, or sad. You might sense that they have a recent bereavement and have some idea of who, such as "They have recently lost a male family member, I think Father". These flashes

of sudden knowingness will be given to you by your Guardian Angel. It is important to learn to trust the intuitive messages that suddenly came from "Nowhere". Naturally, I let a person walk on by. I don't advise talking to someone concerning a message unless, in different settings, they ask for a reading to see if you can pick up an Angel message.

Sensing Angels through our intuition

Have you ever felt that you shouldn't have gone somewhere, and you ignored the feeling? Then something bad happened?

The following is a true account: A lady refused to board a plane to fly on holiday with her husband. They had flown many times before and she wasn't afraid of flying. She had a strong intuitive feeling that something bad was going to happen to the flight. They missed their flight and cancelled their holiday. They heard nothing on the news afterwards, and her husband wasn't happy that their holiday was cancelled. However, they spoke to friends who had taken the same flight. There had been confusion concerning what was happening to the flight amongst passengers. They had experienced severe weather, engine problems, and had to make an emergency landing. Fortunately, no-one was hurt, but it had been a terrifying experience for those on board.

Have you ever met someone you knew whilst in a distant place? Sometimes the Angels steer the timelines of our lives to converge in physical places, perhaps resulting in a meeting that we find helpful to our current life situation.

Have you ever experienced coincidences, the odds of which are happening can be remote? I won't give examples of coincidences. Some are genuine happenings that happen by chance. It is always worth thinking about every coincidence to see if your Guardian Angel is trying to tell you something.

Sensing help from Angels – "Sudden Knowingness"

Have you ever experienced moments of "Sudden Knowingness"?
You might have been wrestling with a problem for some time and then suddenly, as if from nowhere you know what to do.
You might have been in communication with someone and suddenly feel quite strongly that they are mistaken or not telling the truth.
You are planning to travel somewhere and then suddenly get a strong feeling that you will experience some difficulties.
Our Guardian Angels try to guide us. They can often see a way forward through challenges and problems. They communicate their guidance instantly into our mind so effectively that we experience these moments of "Sudden Knowingness". It is always good to trust these intuitive messages. We can learn to trust these as we strengthen our knowledge concerning the Angels.

A Real-Life Example of Sudden Knowingness.
A friend of mine was quite distraught because one of her cats had gone missing. I realised that she lived on a street with many houses around but directed her to the end house where I felt her cat was somehow trapped.
She asked at all the houses, including the end house, and no-one had seen her cat. Several days later her cat was still missing. As a person, just me, I didn't know what to say. Suddenly, my Guardian Angel gave me a vision. I described to her what I saw "Go back to the end house and insist on looking in the rear garden for a side door that leads into a garage. Insist that you look inside. You will not see your cat because he is trapped behind some furniture. He is very weak, but still alive." My friend did exactly as I said. A lady who lives at the end house insisted that she had searched for my friend's cat and that it wasn't there. However, my friend insisted she look in the garage. She saw furniture stored in there but could not see her cat. She then shouted the cat's name, and a feint "Meow" came from behind the furniture. Some furniture had to be partly dismantled to release her cat. He was very weak, but

fortunately has now fully recovered to good health.

How do we Speak to each other in Heaven?

My spiritual research concerning the subject of how we communicate with each other in Heaven led me to a conclusion that this is one of the most important principles to learn and understand in how to sense our Guardian Angels.

In Heaven, although we still retain our individuality, we also realise that we are spiritually connected with each other, with the Angels, and with everyone. We sense a Oneness that is hard to describe.

Communication in Heaven can be with the words of the language that we learnt whilst in physical life. However, we were born out of Heaven as baby without language skills, so how did we communicate before birth? The answer is that communication in Heaven is by projecting our feelings and thoughts. This is the same as the "Instant Knowingness" that I describe as one of the ways our Guardian Angels communicate with us.

In our life as a human being, some people have experiences of "Telepathy". I believe that this isn't a trick of the human brain, but genuinely a moment of spiritual connection with someone else that enables a transfer of thoughts or projection of feelings.

Our thoughts and feelings that we project as a human being are capable of being picked up by Heaven, and by our Guardian Angel. We shouldn't worry about our quiet inner thoughts and feelings because the Angels and Heaven cannot listen to them. Although we might project negative, frustrated, angry thoughts sometimes, it is our actions, not our thoughts, that Heaven sees.

How do we project our thoughts?

In Heaven we project our thoughts and feelings to communicate with other people who have physically died and are now in Heaven nearby. Our Guardian Angel will still be with us, and we will communicate by projecting thoughts and feelings.

When we are born as a baby, we immediately lose the ability to project our thoughts. We have to learn language, but whilst we are learning we are given the instinctive ability to cry when we are hungry, tired, or suffering discomfort. We soon develop an ability to laugh when we are happy.

Once we have learnt how to use language and mathematical skills then these become the primary ways that we project our thoughts. Language can also be expressed by signs made with the hand and face for those with hearing impairment. Language is a projection of some of our thoughts. We need to use the correct words and make the communication more effective using the tone of our voice and perhaps physical expressions. We can show these expressions with our face, our hands, and the stance we take. Do we frown or express anger as we speak loudly, or do we smile and speak gently? Do we get physically closer to someone, or move slightly away? How do we use our hands and arms? Are we pointing at someone, or keeping our hands relaxed?

So, in Heaven we can project our thoughts and feelings instantly and completely. Whilst in physical life as a human being we learn how to project our thoughts through language, tone of voice and body expressions, although this is a slower process than "Instant Knowingness".

Human beings have always sought ever more clever and instant ways to communicate out thoughts, feelings and messages. It cannot be underestimated how important the development of the written word was as a skill that changed our world forever. The ability to write was developed several thousand years ago and it was seen as a miracle. Some learned people in higher developed societies were now able to write their communication in words that could be read exactly word for word, as a story being retold time after time. People in different areas, countries and periods of time could read the same communication of thoughts that the writer put down on stone, paper or parchment. In the early periods of writing only a few people had the opportunity to learn the skills of writing and reading. The countless millions of others who could only hear words been read must have been left with feelings of wonder and awe. Many religions have been founded by the written Word as being itself a miracle of communication. The miracle of the written Word helped people who listened to accept what the written Word was telling them.

Humanity continues to seek better and more rapid means of communication. Perhaps it is the inner memories of Heaven, where communication is instant, that drives humanity on this quest. The internet and world wide web, phone technology, emails, television and social media have transformed communication throughout the world and into our personal lives. Angels are spiritual beings from Heaven, and are a link between us, and Heaven. They still communicate by projection of thoughts and feelings to give us "Instant Knowingness". I hope that humanity can learn to recognise that we cannot always expect words and language messages from Heaven, although the Angels do sometimes communicate with us using words and language.

We need to start to "Sense" the "Projection of Thoughts" messages from the Angels and we can do this by understanding the difference between how Heaven communicates, and how people in life communicate.

Human beings can comminate some of their feelings by projecting them as we do in Heaven. Examples of these are strong feelings of love or anger. This is not as straightforward or easy as it is in Heaven. We can project our feelings of love to someone, and they might pick up these feelings without the need for words. However, the person to whom you project your feeling of love might be blocking you or shielding themselves from sensing any feelings being projected by anyone at them. Some people do this instinctively because it also helps protect them from feelings of anger that are around.

Prayer Works

Having explained how we, and the Angels communicate in Heaven, it might be easier to understand that Prayer is a way of projecting our thoughts and feelings. Our prayers are heard, even if they are projected silently from our mind. To project them is easy, and simply means that we should think of ourselves as talking to someone. That someone being God.

Our prayers, even silent in our minds, are projected thoughts that can be heard by Heaven. We should always pray to the Highest Authority in Heaven whom we believe. I believe in God, so the Highest Authority in my belief is God.

The Angels work in the purpose of Heaven, and although we can thank the Angels, we should always pray to God, and give thanks to God. If our prayer is said with goodness in our soul, then it will be responded to with powerful, positive help from Heaven through the Angels.

As I understand, God doesn't need thanking. However, the process of thanking God, and words of worship help our personal spiritual growth. The reason? Throughout history many, many people have ruled countries, or have been in control of companies, organisations and people and have shown little empathy because they behave as though they themselves are some kind of God.

Whenever we feel our problems are too much for us, or we need healing for ourselves or someone we know, say a prayer to God. The Angels will try to help. I say an inner prayer in my mind many times every day. The Angels respond by helping me through life problems, help to protect me from negative energies, and bring healing and calm. I also pray for life fulfilment and a way forward into the future. I am constantly praying for the world, and others around.

CHAPTER SEVEN

Premonitions

I have now experienced many instances where the Angels have given me visions and messages from Heaven concerning the future. This could be a vision of a future for a person I am helping with an Angel Messages reading, or a premonition concerning a future local, national, or world event. Because everything I do and see is then linked back to my logical research, I believe that it is the correct moment in time to explain this to a wider audience. I believe that the knowledge could make the world a better place as more people seek to learn the enlightenment that can be revealed through this knowledge.

The gifts of Sensing Angels and the ability to receive premonitions are, absolutely, spiritual skills. They are only possible if we can accept that the Spiritual Realm of Heaven is another dimension. It is the familiar home where our soul came from, and where we will return after our physical life on Earth. Until now religious beliefs have made claim to our understanding of the Spiritual Realm. I will not criticise religions for they offer much truth, despite disagreement with one another. However, we do not have to be religious to Sense Angels. Heaven loves us all unconditionally.

Have you ever experienced a premonition? If so, you might not have known how to handle it, or whether to take it seriously. Our modern, materialistic societies don't teach us how to handle premonitions because they are not taken seriously in mainstream belief.

Premonitions concerning happenings in the world

Unlike reading a person's future, premonitions are given to me unannounced, and without prior thoughts of the events in the premonition given to me.

Premonitions work for me in two ways:

1) If a person I am in contact with is to travel somewhere, I might receive a premonition of any serious weather, natural catastrophe, or other personal danger. I also experience such premonitions for myself.

2) I am constantly experiencing premonitions of global events. I was told by my Angel Guide that something big would affect the entire world in 2020. The "Something Big" turned out to be the COVID-19 Pandemic. Climate Change, and the consequences to nature, and our planet is on the minds of many people, and the subject of many of my premonitions.

The following examples are all true accounts of premonitions that came true:

Tsunami

I was given a vision of the Boxing Day Tsunami of December 2004. The vision was given to me six months earlier. I warned a family member not to travel to a beach resort in Thailand because of my visions of a huge wall of water from the sea overwhelming the coastline and going inland. I didn't know what a Tsunami was, but just saw a huge wall of water. My family member listened to the warning that our Guardian Angels had given and said she would think twice about her planned travel to that area. She and

INTUITIVE CLAIRVOYANCE

her husband had spent months training to be diving instructors and were to work for a year as diving instructors for tourists at a holiday beach resort in Thailand. Naturally, they were annoyed at my warnings. Fortunately, for several other reasons they cancelled their plans. Her friends, husband and wife plus a son aged four, had made the same plans, and did journey there. When the Tsunami hit the man was diving underwater, and was swept four miles down the coast, but was uninjured. The woman saved herself and her son by running inland, and she held her son above her head as the water reached shoulder height. Fortunately, they were not injured.

I receive premonitions of danger for myself when I travel. The following true account is just one example.

Bus on fire

It was around 5.30 pm one Spring evening in May 2018, I had to travel home from work by bus because my car was in a garage for repairs. The journey was twelve miles across country from Driffield to Bridlington, Yorkshire. It was a double decker bus, and I was seated downstairs on the left side. I had boarded the bus in Driffield and at the final stop before leaving Driffield I suddenly saw flames rising upwards at the outside of the window alongside of me. Yet, passengers were getting on the bus, obviously not seeing the flames. The flames appeared like those in a cartoon, in full colour orange, yet is if they were drawn by an artist. The vision disappeared as quickly as it came. I didn't know what to do, so I continued my bus journey. Six miles along the road in open countryside the bus suddenly stopped. The engine at the rear had suddenly blown up, with steam and oil everywhere, but no flames. Fortunately, no-one was hurt. I reflected later that I hadn't heeded the warning that my Guardian Angel gave me.

Messages I hear as a voice

I might occasionally hear a spiritual voice from my Guardian Angel when trying to help someone is emotionally stressed.
The voice is always the same, giving me a clear message, but with no emotional expression.

The messages always seem to communicate a healing and happy outcome within four weeks, or in one month. The predicted outcome is almost unbelievable at the time.

Here is a real-life example:

Again, this true account concerns a family member. It was Easter 2019 when I spent several hours trying to console a family member whose fiancée had just left him. They had been in a relationship for seven years, yet she had refused to share a home with him. The relationship seemed to be finished with phone contact and social media contact blocked. I didn't move into psychic mode, and, as most people, I began to feel drained of energy as I tried for several hours to help him feel better, but without success.

I needed a break so went to the bathroom. Suddenly the voice I hear spiritually, speaking with no emotion into my mind said: "She will be back in his life in a full relationship and sharing a home in one month". I went back to join my family member, who was suffering severe depression. How could I tell him about the message? I plucked up the courage and told him. He knows my psychic gift and believes me. He became less depressed, and more positive than he had been all day. One month to the exact day later it transpired that not only were they back together, but she moved in to share a home with him.

I always trust that inner voice. It is the voice of my Guardian Angel, and the Angels can see our future.

The following is a further true account of how some may receive premonitions:

I was giving an Angel messages reading to an elderly lady at her home in the city of Hull. My Angel brought through a vision and messages concerning her father who had been a fisherman on a Hull trawler during his working life. I then brought through a picture of a trawler sinking with loss of life of all those on board.

The lady looked astonished and briefly confirmed the facts, but I asked her not to say anything further.

The Angels then showed me a vision of how her father had refused to board ship one day. He had felt intuitively that something bad was going to happen to the trawler that he worked on. He went home and the trawler set sail without him, never to be return home again due to severe weather.

The lady confirmed everything as true that her deceased father via the Angels had just told me. She then went on to say that he had lived a healthy and full life before he died of natural causes aged in his eighties.

This account shows clearly how many people can receive intuitive feelings. My research show that these are given to us by our Guardian Angels. Some people listen to these feelings and act on them, but many people don't. In this book I explain how important it is for all of us to start to believe in our intuitive feelings and be guided by them throughout life. This is extremely important in helping us to Sense Angels.

CHAPTER EIGHT

Angels Comminication

How Angels Communicate with us.

Angels communicate into our thoughts so completely that we may just take them as being our own thoughts. We have free will. Our inner voice might not even be a voice because it is a series of thoughts that try to warn us and guide us. We constantly create our own thoughts, but the inner voice is different in that the thought, and ideas suddenly come from nowhere. I best describe this as a sudden "knowingness".

With free will, we can choose to ignore our inner voice. If we do this frequently enough then we lose our close relationship with our Guardian. We may then become reckless in our actions, and inconsiderate, lacking in empathy for other people, and for animals, nature and the environment.

We may have spiritual callings such as charity work, concern for animals, concern for nature, concern for the planet. When we balance our free will thoughts with our inner voice from our Guardian then our spiritual callings will bear fruit. We can and do generate our own love for others, and we have our own skills and abilities.

Guardian Angels are a part of our conscience. Our conscience is within our inner self and may whisper to us that something we have done, or are considering doing may hurt someone, or hurt an animal, or hurt nature.

Some people become so self-centred that they never listen to their Guardian Angel.
In such cases their Guardian is unable to give thought into the minds of these people that act as their conscience. Eventually this cutting off from their Guardian is so total that they no longer hear the inner voice. Their Guardian cannot get through to them. Such people might seem to be civilised and confine their self-centred actions to walking over others legally in business, career, or relationships. They, and others can, and do hurt people physically or mentally without feeling guilty.

Negative, earthbound spirits of evil energies cannot get inside anyone who has still a connection with their Guardian Angel. Our Guardians protect us from negative energies. The earth plane does have a lot of negative energy. Spirits who are evil can still be bound to the earth plane and seek opportunities to target individuals who have torn away from their Guardian. Negative, evil spirits can then try to communicate directly into their thoughts. If such a person has a dark character, it is easy for the evil spirit to stoke their fire of self-centred purpose to cause harm. This type of person goes out and does harm to others and has no conscience concerning harming animals and nature.
Our Guardians work through our intuition, giving sudden answers to problems, feelings inside about what to do. These seem to come from nowhere. An impossible overpowering problem can suddenly be answered by seeing what to do.

Spiritual Talents
Our Guardian Angels can almost become one with us, melding into our being, when we are using our spiritual talents to help others, help animals, help nature or work to help the

environment. This "As one" feeling may produce a totality of our inner strength, determination, and spiritual powers to enable us to do the work.

I firmly believe that many scientific discoveries have been inspired inside the thoughts of our great scientists by their Guardians as part of some Higher Plan.

Our Guardian Angels can also work externally in helping these things around happen in a better way for you.

Angels can help us achieve that deep-down longing for fulfilment that most of us yearn. We all have different talents and ability, and our Guardians can help us make the most of what we have got.

The most successful people achieve their ambitions and personal goals through being totally focused. They have tunnel vision and imagine where they want to be and what they want to achieve. If their vision is good, and will cause no hurt or harm, then they will be helped by listening closely to the inner voice from their Guardian Angel. People are mostly unaware that their own thoughts and visions can be enhanced by their Guardian, who may feed them ideas, inspiration, motivation and positive energy along the way.

Yes, our Guardians feed us many differing kinds of positive spiritual Energy!

Guardian Angels are Beings of Unconditional Love from the Spiritual Realm of Heaven and will never put thoughts in people's minds that will cause hurt or harm in any way.

OUR GUARDIAN ANGELS CHANNEL HEALING TO US

Amazing reports of significant healing benefits have been received from people who have received healing from the Heaven via the Angels

INTUITIVE CLAIRVOYANCE

Healing can be towards a quicker recovery from illness, to ease the pain of stress or bereavement, or to ease depression.

Healing can be to our lives, to provide a happier and brighter future and personal fulfilment through greater success in whatever we do.

You may think "I don't often need healing, for I am generally in good health".

Alternatively, you may think "I don't have a Guardian Angel healing me, for I am always unwell".

Our Guardian Angels constantly bring healing to us

Our human body is frail in this harsh world we live in. It is a miracle that we can survive with such a fragile body, constantly at risk from injury and accident, and constantly exposed to germs that cause illness.

Many people damage their health through bad diet, smoking, drinking alcohol, lack of exercise. Our Guardian Angels are constantly working to help us when our free will actions are harming our bodies

That miracle is the constant work by our Guardian Angels, healing, protecting, guiding us away from danger, and trying to keep our immune systems, and other bodily defences at optimum efficiency.

LIFE ENERGIES

Our Guardian Angels channel Healing Life Energies into us.

The time when I most often see Angels is when their energies are intensified in channelling healing to other people.

Life Energies can be a shade of purple, pure healing energy, Springtime light green for renewing body cells, and Golden for pure Life Energy, plus many other shades of the colour spectrum.

The following is a true account:

A was giving a lady an Angel messages reading, and the Angels gave me some meaningful messages from her grandma, who had raised her throughout childhood, and had been a loving mother because her real mother had left the family for another relationship. Towards the end of the reading, I was given a message that she was in severe pain with her left knee. She confirmed what I said and told me that she was to have a knee operation, to fit a replacement knee, the next day. I asked her if she would like some spiritual healing and she agreed.

When I channel Angel healing, it is non-contact. I hold my hand a few centimetres away from a person's forehead and talk though what happens. I immediately saw several healing Angels come in close. One Angel projected a blue energy to bring pain relief and ease the inflammation around her knee area. Another brought in a Springtime green energy to help renewal of the damaged cells in her muscles and tendons. A beautiful purple energy came in to bring powerful healing to her. I could see the Angels shimmering with the colour of the Life Energies they channelled.

The lady became very relaxed and started to feel well as the pain disappeared.

I saw the lady a few weeks later. She was walking without pain, and excited to tell me that the knee replacement operation had gone exceptionally well, and she had made a recovery much quicker than her surgeon had expected. She commented that she was convinced that this was due to the powerful benefit of the healing she had received from the Angels.

Another true account

I gave an Angel messages reading to a young woman who was pregnant, but her personal health was damaged by an extremely bad "Junk Food" diet, smoking, drinking alcohol etc. Her baby was subsequently born perfect. I am not a medical person but know enough about the human body to realise that our cells need the correct nutrition, trace elements, proteins, that are the building blocks of life. I am certain many of you reading this will have known a mother with similar lifestyle, although I realise that babies can be born with health problems from mothers who don't take care of their personal health.

I asked my Guardian Angel: "How can the baby have such perfection?" My Guardian replied: "Through invisible Life Energy the Healing Angels can channel into a baby in the womb the building blocks of Life that people might truly believe can only come from nutrients in food, or from the mother"

Intuition

Our Guardian Angels work through our intuition, giving sudden answers to problems, and feelings inside about what to do. These seem to come from nowhere. An impossible overpowering problem can be answered by suddenly seeing what needs to be done.

Angels communicate into our thoughts so completely that we just take them as being our own thoughts.

Conscience

Our Guardian Angels work through our conscience so strongly that my research indicates our conscience may be up to 100% our Guardian Angel.

As human beings we all have the gift of Free Will. It seems that our Guardian Angels cannot prevent us from making our Free Will decisions in everyday life. What they can and do is to put feelings into our minds that we commonly describe as our "Conscience". These feelings are like an inner voice, urging us not to do something that may hurt others.

Many of our actions in life impact directly on others. If our actions in some way cause hurt to others, either emotionally, psychologically, or physically then our conscience should make us aware of this. We may question our conscience and say: "Well, I know a person, or other people may not like what I intend to do, but it is for "Good" in the long-term."

Alternatively, we may just go-ahead and do things which hurt others in some way, and our actions are for our own self-centred needs and satisfaction.

Our conscience should always tell us if we are doing something spiritually wrong.

Some people are so self-centred that they always ignore their conscience. Eventually they lose their conscience completely. Their Guardian Angel cannot get through.
Something new starts to happen. When a Guardian Angel stands back because someone is totally self-centred and is going through life hurting others, then it leaves a spiritual void. The void is caused because the Guardian Angel has had to stand back, cannot get through and cannot protect the individual from negative, evil energies.

Negative energies are always around waiting on the earth plane, waiting for an opportunity to get into someone who is no longer protected by their Guardian Angel.
Once negative energy starts to influence a person then their evil actions towards others become more intense and more frequent.

Spiritual Gifts
We all have some Spiritual Gift. It is better not to envy or be jealous about someone else's spiritual gift, but to try to identify our gift, and make the most of it.
We may have spiritual gifts such as a need to help others, concern for animals, concern for nature, concern for the planet. When we balance our free will thoughts with our inner voice from our Guardian then our spiritual gifts will bear fruit. We can and do generate our own love for others, and we have our own skills and abilities.
People who have an inner driving force that helps others, or helps nature, or helps the environment can be classed as having a spiritual gift.

Guardian Angels help us when we work to help others
Our Guardian Angel will help us with our work, and at times almost become one with us in terms of spiritual energy and

purpose. At such times we will care less about ourselves, other than keeping ourselves healthy, and be almost totally dedicated to the purpose of helping others.

Problems and Guidance

Angels communicate into our thoughts so completely that we just take them as being our own thoughts.

We have free will. Our inner voice is not even a voice but thoughts that warn us, guide us. Don't get me wrong, we constantly create our own thoughts. The inner voice is different in that the thought, and ideas suddenly come from nowhere. I best describe this as a sudden "knowingness".

With Free Will we can choose to ignore our inner voice. If we do this frequently enough then we lose our close relationship with our Guardian. We may then become reckless in our actions, and inconsiderate, lacking in empathy for other people for animals, nature and the environment.

Real Life Examples of how our Guardian Angels Guide Us

Self: "I want to earn a lot of money. I will earn money by becoming a pop star or successful actor"

Guardian: "These are not your talents. Don't try to be something you haven't the talent for."

Focus on what you feel from your Guardian you can do, try hard, and be a success!

Self: "I am out shopping but don't know where to go for a gift for my family member/ friend. I am getting stressed and tired."

Guardian: "Just blank your thoughts, slow down. You will suddenly know which shop to go into and be drawn to a suitable gift." This is your Guardian at work!

A "Calling"

Ever wondered why some people are so determined to do something to help others? Why some people are determined to work helping animals, nature, or the environment?

I believe that many people are given a "Calling". This is a gift from

Heaven to do a particular task. The task is part of a Divine Plan to make sure that every aspect of life has people interested in caring and working to cherish, protect, repair and bring healing.

Our Guardian Angels know this Divine Plan and work to help those with a Calling to help them fulfil their inner driving force to care for other people, or care for animals, nature, and planet Earth. Our Guardian Angels Can Give Us Special Help.

At times we may need special help in life.

For ourselves we may need special healing in times of health crises.
We may need extra help through difficult situations.
For others we may wish for urgent healing when seriously ill or injured. For others we may wish for their lives to be urgently improved from bad situations.

How Can We Ask for Special Help?
We ask for Special Help through Prayer. Yes, prayer either in our thoughts, or out loud. Prayer alone, or in unison and harmony with others.
Our thoughts and prayers are heard in Heaven because Heaven is a place of pure thought.
How do we Pray?
We should never pray to our Guardian Angels. They work in the purpose of God, and on the instructions of God.
We should always pray to God. Pray upwards to the Highest Spiritual Authority, to God, and the powerful, loving actions needed to answer our prayer will be passed back down to our Guardian Angels.

ANGELS HELP US TOWARDS OUR DREAMS OF FUTURE ACHIEVEMENT

Firstly: What is your vision of what you want for the future? Are such dreams positive and good?
Secondly: What talents and abilities do you have? What talents

and abilities don't you have?
Thirdly: You can fight through disability. You can fight through being in the wrong part of society. You can fight through lack of academic ability or achievement. You can fight through having no start-up money.
Fourthly: You will find it harder in a society that suppresses people. Your dreams must be realistic within the society you live.
Our Guardians work through our dreams. Not all the time. When a dream seems REAL then it will be real.
Our Guardian Angels are of the Spiritual Realm and can link our soul to Heaven whilst we are in dream state. This might be to link to loved ones who have passed. I have heard many people tell me how they experienced dreams that seemed like real life with their husband/wife/parents who had passed.

Dreams frequently give us mixed visions of our life events that are difficult to interpret. Our physical brain replays current life experiences, and these can be mixed with spiritual visions from our Guardians.
Dreams are taken seriously by many people.

FREE WILL: THE MOST DIFFICULT PART OF OUR PERSON

Angels stand back when our Free Will is driven by self-centred behaviour that will hurt others.
We are all given a life for an important purpose. That purpose is to spiritually grow.
Our life on Earth as human beings is a transient experience.
We are in Heaven before we are born, and we return to Heaven at the end of physical life.
We are given life to experience being human. Interaction with others in our relationships with people is a massive part of that experience. We are given life for learning, for adventure, for the physical experiences of walking, running free, sport, and competition.

We seek to find love again, as we experienced in Heaven, where love is the air that we breathe. We may find love in our mother's arms as a baby. We seek love in our relationships as we grow older. Sometimes such love can be confusing because it is tainted by desire.

The true unconditional love from Heaven is still with us through our Guardian Angel. If we recognise our Guardian Angel as close to us, then we may feel that love with us most of the time. If we choose by our Free Will to distance ourselves from our Guardian Angel, then we may feel cold and isolated inside.

Free Will is given to us because as spiritual beings we are respected by Heaven.

We can choose to do what we want in life, but often our Free Will urges may knock us off the path of our Life Plan. Things go wrong and we wonder why.

The most destructive parts of Free Will become apparent when we choose to ignore our Guardian Angel. Many of the populations of the world are not even aware of their Guardian Angels, so Free Will choices are made without this high level of awareness. Often, we find people acting in a self-centred way, not caring too much if they hurt others emotionally, psychologically, or physically.

Through their Free Will many people inadvertently or deliberately go against all the ways their Guardian Angels try to Guide them. These ways are through a person's conscience, intuition, and caring thoughts. On far too many occasions Guardian Angels are forced to stand back, for such is the gift of Free Will that we are allowed to prioritise the decisions we make for ourselves, even when we cause harm.

Negative energy is not far away in all our lives. The world is constantly generating all kinds of spiritual energy from the vast number of spirits in the form of living people that are currently in life.

Love is the strongest, most powerful energy of all, constantly battling against the negative, evil energies in our physical universe.

If people, through their Free Will, choose to act in a self-centred way that may hurt other people, or hurts nature or the environment in a big way then their Guardian Angel cannot get through. The tragedy is that negative entities might then see an opportunity to get through into the minds of these people. This makes their self-centred behaviour move in the direction of evil. This is a big subject!

I can describe to people I read through the visions Angels give me of their personal future, but with the ability to help them change their future to be happy and fulfilling. This is an important factor because we all could change our futures if we learn to recognise and accept spiritual guidance that can be available for us every minute of every day.

Guardian Angels are working through many, many people via their intuition, to give them a "Calling" to help during a pandemic, and longer-term to avert the more serious consequences of Climate Change. That is why some people seem extremely dedicated to this work.

We need to educate the world concerning the spiritual guidance that can be sought concerning real ways and actions to avoid the serious consequences of climate change.

CHAPTER NINE

Angels can give us Visions

As an example of the Angels giving me visions of the future on an individual basis the following is a true account of a reading that involved seeing the future for a lady. Without her telling me anything beforehand, I discovered in the reading that her family were deeply troubled by what had happened to their son. During the reading I saw two outcomes for their son, one good, and one not so good, so I focussed on the good path, and the future changed as I spoke to become the better outcome.

The lady sitting in front of me screamed. Her scream shook the house and surely neighbours would come running in to see what had happened. I was a stranger who had been sat facing this lady across a kitchen table for no more than five minutes. Her scream shook me with an unexpected shudder of sudden stress because I am not the kind of guy who does anything to make women scream. I am a clairvoyant and she had booked me to visit her home to give her a reading. This lady was aged around 40 years and was obviously taking no care of her appearance with greasy hair all over the place, and scruffy clothes. She seemed depressed as she welcomed me into her house and sat me down.
My first words that I was given by my Angel Guide were simply "It's about Justice – or rather an injustice – your son is in prison

for an offence he didn't commit" That is when she screamed. I had visualised some heavy-weight fighter of a husband appearing and throwing me out, but fortunately she had kicked him out of the house for a few hours for privacy during the reading. What I told her was correct, but then I went on to tell her that her son's prison sentence would be overturned, and he would be a free man within four weeks. Her scream was of surprise at how I could possibly know all of this. I spent another hour with her, bringing-in some quite clear messages from her deceased mother. She calmed down very quickly and became more optimistic and much happier over that hour, and the messages from her mum appeared to be of great meaning. I left her with good wishes, inside my mind saying a quiet prayer for her and her son.

This was in the city of Hull, which I only visit several times a year, and I never go to the public houses there. However, about a month later I did call into a Hull pub with some friends, but in a different area of the city. Hull is a big place. Within minutes an attractive lady came running up to me and gave me a big hug saying: "It's him… it's him…". I couldn't help but notice a rather tough looking partner behind her looking quite angry at her behaviour. "It's ok," she told him. "This is the clairvoyant". The partner changed his mood, put a smile on his face and shook my hand. "Our son is no longer in prison, everything you said came true". The fact that their son was now free was good news, but the added miracle for me was the transformation of this lady. She had taken on a new zest for living, pulled herself out of depression, and acquired a new interest in taking care of herself. She had given herself a makeover with her hair and dress, with such a dramatic improvement that I hadn't recognised her immediately. This was the miracle of what clairvoyance can offer. I have witnessed this miracle many times as people take their lives off "hold" and start living again. My friends in the pub had been staring-on in amazement. I didn't openly discuss my work in giving people messages via the Angels. One of my hobbies is singing, and we had just done a concert, so my fellow singers in the pub knew nothing about me sensing Angels. I just tried to shoulder-off what had happened in a joking way.

CHAPTER TEN

OUR GUARDIAN ANGELS KNOW OUR FUTURE

When I am giving someone a reading my Guardian Angel works with their Guardian Angel. Our Guardian Angels know our Life Plan and know some of our future.

Guardian Angels won't let us see all the future. There are good reasons for this, but they will allow us an insight into some of our future.

They almost always have been many years trying to "Get Through" to the person by trying to guide them by giving them intuitive feelings every step of the way. However, in this modern materialistic world we are told that spiritual things aren't real, including the existence of Angels, so many people never listen to their intuition.

Working with the Angels on our Life Plan can help change our future for the better!

When I give someone a Life Plan reading, if the Angels are willing to help then some amazing visions unfold before my spiritual eye. I am usually shown two versions of the future, two paths for someone. The first path is a future that would happen anyway, without my intervention. It usually has the same difficulties and challenges that a person has experienced in life up to the present, continuing as before.

The second version of the future is a path of greater happiness, life fulfilment, fewer things going wrong. I choose not to dwell on the first path, so I describe the happier, more fulfilling second path to the person I am giving a reading to.

The miracle is that as I describe the second path the Angels are working to change the person's future for the better. The second happier, more fulfilling path becomes their new future.

The moment in time that the Angels reveal an in-depth Life Plan is the pivotal moment in a person's life that changes their future for the better!

I have helped many thousands of people free of charge over the past 15 years, using my clairvoyant gift.

My Spiritual Research is based on logical conclusions, and a belief in an amazing intelligence within the spiritual dimension that communicates through the Angels.

I am constantly guided by the Angels who work in unconditional love, and I always work using my spiritual gift of Discernment. This is the true ability to discern between good and evil. Opening oneself up to spiritual messages and visions from Heaven is risky because any enhanced spiritual awareness can also open ourselves up to the heavy negative, evil spiritual energies that are earthbound. The ability to discern comes with the knowledge that negative energies can be blocked, instructed to go away, and even dealt with by prayer. I often pray for the Angels that I call "Rescue Angels" to carry away earthbound souls to a place where they can find peace.

In addition to being given visions of the future for some people, I may also receive other messages from Heaven, through the Angels. These have been given to me over many years.

The messages are about the meaning of life and have revealed an amazing picture. This has helped me to help others which is absolutely the reason why I have been given this work.

Our future is not just simply knowing what our personal future may become but being aware that the Angels can change some of our personal future to maximise our happiness and fulfilment.

LIFE LESSONS

Our Life Plan was determined before we were born: What we would do, where we would live, people we would form a relationship with, including soulmates.

We may find ourselves making the same mistakes over, and over again. In human relationships, career, personal-finance, and all aspects of our lives. We may be told that is the fault of our Free Will, but often we seem slow to learn. Sometimes the real reason is because of our Life Lessons.

Life Lessons are worked-out and planned before we are born. These can be identified through a heightened awareness as we learn to Sense Angels. Life Lessons can also be identified by recognising the life experience of recurring unfair, difficult times such as in relationship problems.

Once our Life Lessons are identified we can change our outlook on how we tackle the future. Life lessons do not include serious illness or accident. These events are not on our life plan. The way that we can avoid these is to learn to listen to spiritual warnings that we are given through our feelings, primarily our intuition.

Free Will

A lot of weight is given to Free Will steering our lives. It certainly influences our everyday routine decision-making.

We may also be surrendering some of our Free Will to others, such as when we are in a personal relationship.

No matter what our Free Will does for us, or which way it leads us, our positive Life Plan events will still happen.

Future global events such as severe weather events and natural disasters can be seen through Angel visions at a personal level if that person is to travel to the affected area. Warnings can be given to avoid the situation.

SIXTH SENSE

The understanding of how and why the future can be partly seen has been a significant part of my spiritual research project over the last 40 years. Some people claim to have a "Sixth Sense". This is the ability to sense spiritually and is our Guardian Angel at work. Our Sixth Sense can give us feelings about the future.

When I give an Angel messages reading, it is often to help a grieving relative with a loved one who has passed.
However, many more people want to know what the future holds for them, and the ability to help people see some of the future is an important part of my work.
The Spiritual Realm is a place of Unconditional Love.
We may travel through life worried about the future, and sometimes feeling cold inside, because we are not feeling the love from our Guardian Angels. The society we live in does not teach how to recognise our Guardian Angels. I can show you how to reconnect with their spiritual love and guidance that will lead us to true happiness and fulfilment.

LOGICAL EXPLANATIONS

Logical discoveries through Spiritual Research are mostly not capable of being proven by science, simply because science, especially physics, is based entirely on the way our physical universe is put together. The Spiritual Realm is another dimension, with its own building blocks that cannot be measured by our physics. Both our universe, and the spiritual dimension have one major thing in common, and that is immense energy. I personally believe that, just like weighing scales, the energy of our physical universe is in balance with the energy of the spiritual dimension.

FIRST HEAVEN

As described earlier, there are many people who have had "Near Death Experiences" (NDE), and for those who wish further reading there are many books, and YouTube videos where you can see personal stories of such experiences.
The Angels have helped me see through to the beautiful place that many who have an "NDE" travel to. I call this place "First Heaven". Why? Because it is the first place most of us go when we first leave our Earthly life. It is a very real, solid place, and created in the image of the Earthly home we have just left so that we can transition into the next life. There are valleys, rivers, lakes, trees, flowers, green grass. Colours are vivid and the experience of being in that place is intense and joyful. Others who have passed may be waiting to greet us, but only where there is a bond of love or warm friendship. Dogs, cats, horses, can be seen with those who cared for them in life.
We can stay in this place for a long time, although there is no real time, but only the moment of "Now".
We will then move on to further experiences, and ultimately to be reborn into another life.

REINCARNATION

It would seem that we all have many lives. Each life is given to us for adventure, experience, challenges, and hopefully spiritual growth.
How do we achieve spiritual growth?
We grow spiritually when we become less self-centred, and more caring towards other people, towards animals, nature and the environment.
To spiritually grow is why we have many lives, and our Life Plan

is reset before each life to improve on our previous lives. Our Guardian Angels know our Life Plan.

WHO ARE WE?

We are an immortal soul. Our soul energy cannot be seen because it is made of the same stuff as energies within the spiritual realm. Over many years of giving clairvoyant readings, I see that we retain our memories, and our character when we leave our physical body and pass back home to Heaven at the end of our physical life. Our soul, the person we are, the "I", the "Me" inside each one of us is eternal.

What do those in Heaven know about our future?

Heaven is a place of infinite intelligence. We all have a Life Plan that was determined for us before we were born. Those in Heaven know our Life Plan. Those in Heaven who are closest to us in our daily lives are our Guardian Angels.

Our Life Plan would include the major events planned for our life such as whom we might meet, the work we will do, and the interests we might pursue, plus much more. When fortune tellers pick up future happenings in a person's life these are the things they might pick up. However, other things are also planned for our lives before we are born, and fortune tellers often miss these. I call them "Life Challenges". Such challenges can be hard, difficult, and make life a struggle for long periods of time. They are put in place to give us life experience, adventure, and with a purpose of helping us spiritually grow more rapidly. Spiritual Growth means to become more caring towards others, towards animals and nature, and towards the environment of our planet Earth. Those who have an inner drive, a Calling, to do what they can to reduce the effects of climate change are an example of human beings caring about our planet Earth, and the future of humanity, and nature.

Those in Heaven are living in a place of beauty, unconditional love, purpose, and oneness. This "Oneness" means that all knowledge, and everything about us, is known, and we, the person inside who we call "I" or "Me" is made of the same Conscious soul energy as the souls in Heaven.

So, what do our Guardian Angels know of our personal future? Well, firstly they know our Life Plan and Life Challenges. Some of the Life Plan and challenges will have already happened and are now in the past. You may want a better future, and my teachings will help identify the past events that have been difficult, and then help to identify your future, and change it towards a better course, giving you potential for greater happiness and fulfilment.

Our Guardian Angels allow us to see some of the future that has already been planned, but not everything. To pick up what they are prepared to show us concerning our personal future we need to learn how to live our lives feeling and resonating more closely with them. I have devoted an entire chapter of this book to help you learn to identify and work with your Guardian Angel. This is extremely important in my teachings, and if you follow it through this alone may change your life in a positive way forever!

The infinite intelligence of Heaven includes a knowingness of what everyone is doing. Imagine some huge computer program that combines events and stores the information of over seven billion people so that it can give the intelligent loving Source in Heaven, whom religions may call "God", a picture of the future.
The Source can also see events happing in nature, and to planet Earth. We may be given some of this picture, but only as they think we need, via our Guardian Angels. This view of the future will come as "Premonitions". The world will become a better and safer place if human beings could universally accept the existence of our Guardian Angels, and then learn how to listen to them.

What spoils the plan, and what makes the world so blind? The answer is negative energy. The human beings who are totally self-centred, and totally lacking in empathy for other people, and for animals, nature, and the environment, are totally disconnected from their personal Guardian Angel. Guardian Angels resonate closely with us when we are caring and loving and will not help us if we are self-centred.

Those in Heaven can see what people who are filled with negative, self-centred energy. Heaven can see what they are doing, and what they are likely to do. Those in Heaven cannot get through to such people because the main channel of communication is through our Guardian Angels.

Those in Heaven therefore get through to people who are resonating more closely with their Guardian Angels, to give them feelings, awareness, and a "Calling" to do what they can to work against the destruction caused by the self-centred ones.

If self-centred behaviour is at the heart of those in government of a nation, then everyone suffers. Alternatively, if those in government have policies of care towards others then many of the citizens of a nation will have more personal freedom, and a better quality of life.

CHAPTER ELEVEN

Discovering the Meaning of Life

Most human beings have their own spiritual beliefs. However, if you wish to learn how to sense Angels it means learning the "System" of how the Spiritual Realm works, as I teach. My ability to sense Angels came to me inadvertently following many years of research into the meaning of life. These same discoveries have withstood the test of time for me and have proven essential to my ongoing understanding of the spiritual visions and messages that I receive.

I urge you to understand this "System", and I feel that as you assimilate this knowledge you may begin to understand the true "Bigger Picture" and start to "Open-up" clairvoyantly.

For me personally, understanding the System is an absolute in my interpreting the visions that I experience. The Spiritual System has been the subject of my research for more than 40 years. Sometimes the visions the Angels give me are powerful, sometimes faint. The energies that I perceive can overwhelm the senses or be faint energies at the extreme periphery of perception. By understanding the System, I know what the Angels are trying to communicate. The meaning and significance of visions can be interpreted and made sense of correctly.

The System Outline

There are two main universes: the physical universe, and the spiritual universe of the Heavens. Their energies balance each other.

The spiritual universe has its own laws of physics that cannot be detected by the science of our physical universe.

The spiritual universe is an almost infinite, vast energy, and is a conscious intelligence. I call it the dimension of "Conscious Energy".

Our soul, the person we call "I" or "Me", is made of conscious energy. Our true home is in Heaven.

There is a vast intelligence at the centre of the spiritual universe, a source of all creation and purpose. We are born out of this "Source" (whom religions may name "God").

When we are in the spiritual universe the energy that we feel, almost like air that we breathe, is that of unconditional love.

We will live through many lives over thousands of years. The purpose of each life is for adventure, experience, and to spiritually grow more caring and loving of other souls, and Creation. We eventually end up merging back into the Source.

There are many Angels in the spiritual universe of the Heavens. Angels have many different roles. Their purpose is to help care for us, and for nature, and for the planet.

We each have at least one Angel dedicated to helping us. We can describe such Angels as "Guardian Angels" or "Angel Guides".

After each life we have a period of spiritual rest, and a life review. We may stop for many years (although there is no time in the spiritual universe) and look over those still in life whom we love.

At some point it will be necessary to move on within the spiritual realm, probably in readiness for being born again into a new life.

Before each life, we are given a "Life Plan". A Life Plan will include things we will do in life, people we will meet, plus much more. We are also set "Life Challenges". Such challenges will be difficult, but we will learn much from the experiences, and hopefully become a better person.

After we are born, our memory of Heaven is forgotten, and our Life Plan, and Life Challenges are not held in our conscious mind. However, our Guardian Angels know these plans and challenges, and will try to help us throughout life. The secret is learning to be closer to our Guardian Angels so that we can sense the help they try to give us.

Our Angels try to help people in the following ways:
They are a link between ourselves and our loved ones in Heaven
They are a channel for healing
They know our life situation, and will try to help and guide us
They know some of our future, and will allow us to see some of our future
They may bring us premonitions concerning the future.

My early spiritual experiences

Have you ever had a spiritual experience and perhaps a sense of your Guardian Angel? This can sometimes happen when we are seriously ill and near death. I describe my own experience of being with my Guardian Angel in Heaven whilst I was fighting for life in hospital.

A ten-month old baby struggling for life with severe life-threatening asthma could be observed lying in a cot in an oxygen tent. The location was a hospital in the city of Bradford, Yorkshire, England. The year was 1951.

The baby was me, and up to the age of 10 months I had been a healthy baby but having been given a childhood vaccine the day before, I now had suffered an immune system reaction, and started with severe asthma that could not be brought under control.

The police officer knocked loudly on the front door of a Victorian terrace house in the city of Bradford, Yorkshire, England, and the city was enveloped by a heavy fog of mist and smoke from the industry powered by coal, coal fires warming the houses, and the local chimneys of cotton mills and woollen mills. The locals gave a name for this pollution as "Smog".
It was late evening, and a young couple apprehensively opened the door to a male police officer who said, "We have just received a call from the hospital. Your baby son is near death and won't survive the night". Very few people had a home telephone in 1951. Telephones were a luxury of the wealthy, very few people owned a car, and in the years soon after World War Two most people didn't have many of the things that we take for granted in the 21st century.
The young couple were my parents, and I was the baby. I had been a fit and healthy baby, but a diphtheria vaccination triggered severe asthma which hospitalised me, leaving me struggling for life lying in a cot in an oxygen tent.
My parents were only allowed to visit once weekly, and then only to observe me through a glass window to help prevent infection. This appeared to be the procedure throughout my time in hospital – over eighteen months. The police called at my parents' home on several occasions throughout that period because I was near to death.

My parents caught the first bus available next morning to the hospital, feeling distraught, only to find with joy and much emotion that I had made a significant recovery and was no longer in danger.
This was the first time that I had been close to death, but I continued to have recurrent severe asthma attacks with all the crisis that an asthma attack brings.

Do infants remember their lives at such a young age? My detailed memory of all this is not there, but I do clearly remember times when I was no longer in my body but in a warm secure

INTUITIVE CLAIRVOYANCE

loving place with a loving spiritual being. My speech as an infant wasn't fully developed but the feelings were that I was rescued from my suffering body and had spent a lot of time with this beautiful being. I was then sent back to my body and immediately experienced the suffering again. I remember feeling "I don't want to go back", only to be told "You have to go back".
Looking back on this time now, I realise that the beautiful loving being is my Guardian Angel. We all have a Guardian Angel, and in this book, I will explain how these beautiful beings stay with us and try to help us throughout our lives and beyond this life.

What were my memories of this time? I remember being with a loving Angel figure, no wings, just a beautiful loving being who cared for me. Most of the time I felt no suffering, but existed in a secure place, surrounded by love. I knew I was somewhere else, not in the body of that suffering infant. I didn't want to go back into my body, but somehow, I had to. There was no language in communicating this to me, just feelings, just a "Knowingness".
I was left with permanent asthma. I would get frequent attacks, and symptoms became acute with exercise, so I could never participate in sport. I missed half of my school life and was always a sickly child. However, like many people with a disability, I eventually became more determined to succeed than most, and achieved high grades in school, before leaving in my mid-teens to pursue a career in accountancy.
Throughout my childhood the experience of being with my Guardian Angel, and still feeling my Guardian Angel with me was constant. I failed to understand violence. Why do some children start fights and cause hurt? Why does it give some children pleasure to bully others? Why do children cause psychological hurt to others by calling them names? Why do children and adults cause pain to others – isn't there enough pain in daily survival?
Of course, I understand now that much of this behaviour is a part of growing up, but such behaviour for many, many people is still there in adulthood. We live in a world that is advanced in science but suffers much spiritually primitive behaviour caused by many

adults. Often those in positions of power and authority have attained their positions by walking over others. Alternatively, authority and leadership can, of course, be attributed to "Survival of the fittest". This would imply that spiritual forces at work might intend that to happen.

However, throughout my childhood, into adult life, and still to this day I realise two things:

1) Sometimes we cannot help hurting others – life throws situations at us daily. How we react and respond can never be perfect.

2) Should we deliberately hurt others, if we are too self-centred and have little empathy for others, then this causes hurt and is spiritually wrong.

My awareness of Guardian Angels opened a door to my spiritual senses and my enhanced intuitive feelings became a normal part of my life.

However, living in a modern world of science, materialism, and new technological advances, I found conflict with my spiritual experiences. My logical mind had to find proof of my spirituality. I am an accountant, I have a car, computers, and immerse myself fully in the world around.

Of course, I was born into a world where science rules. Historically science and religion have been at total odds with each other. I use the word "Religion" because almost all spiritual beliefs are classified as either "Religious beliefs and experiences" being good, and every other spiritual experience as being bad.

THE ARCHANGEL

On a beautiful Spring morning, 1st May 1999 I awoke at 6am to find sunshine penetrating the curtains.

As I lay resting in bed, realising this was a Saturday morning and thinking that I don't have to get up for work, something wonderful happened. A spiritual face appeared in front of me. The face was that of an Archangel. I felt fearful, but then a reassuring feeling came across from this incredible Being who was radiating golden light. His face was itself a golden light. The eyes were what drew my attention. A feeling that He knew everything about me, but understood, and that He forgave my mistakes and imperfections. His love was, and is, unconditional.

This book isn't about religion. I am a Christian, having been baptised in the Church of England as a baby and then baptised again with a fundamental Church in Keighley, Yorkshire at the age of 19 years. For most of my life I hadn't attended Church, but still tried to live a Christian lifestyle. Although I knew I had some "Sixth Sense", I had always been very sceptical of clairvoyants, mediums, psychics, and fortune tellers. Firstly, Christians don't approve of what they do. Secondly my logical mind simply thought of them as nonsense. This same logical mind had spent a lifetime trying to find the meaning of life. Although by profession I am an accountant, I had made an amateur study of astronomy, astrophysics, and quantum physics. I subscribed to the magazine "New Scientist", avidly devouring the latest scientific discoveries and theories. I had studied religious beliefs. I loved nature. Dogs, cats, horses, rabbits, birds, all animals to me seemed to have someone inside looking out. It isn't just human beings who have a soul. The trees, flowers, plants, and all of nature, seem to vibrate with a life-giving energy from a divine source. Equally importantly I had also listened to people. I listened to real life experiences. So many ordinary people over the years would recount their own real-life experiences of ghosts. On every occasion I was always very willing to listen because to me there was a need to evaluate the situation. Old ladies would tell me how they knew their deceased husband was still close by. All of these things are spiritual experiences that Christians must deny. All these things are largely ignored by many people in modern, scientific, materialistic societies. They think about education, career, work, family, things to buy, holidays, sport. All these are good, normal things. All are a part of life. Then when someone they know and love passes from life they are thrown into a desolate place of grief and loss, with no answers from anyone.

What is it all about?

So now, here I am, lying in bed with the face of a Heavenly Being, an Archangel, in front of me. I heard no words but just knew instantly what I was being told. I suddenly felt myself rising-up at great speed to enter a new dimension and saw before me a beautiful place. "This is First Heaven" was the knowledge implanted in my thoughts. What I saw before me I will now describe.

Firstly, I will describe the feelings. At first, I sensed a pleasant caressing feeling of gentle warmth. This grew quickly into a feeling of love. Yes, I could FEEL love as something tangible. I realised that love was all around just like the air we breathe. I felt at ease in this relaxed atmosphere of love. I began to understand this was what some people describe as "Unconditional Love". I felt important and loved even though I knew I was far from perfect.

This new dimension is very real. I could see a rock-solid landscape of a green valley before my eyes. It struck me how vivid the colours hit my vision everywhere I turned, with vivid shades of green grass, the leaves of trees, and every shade of flower vibrating in the beauty and aura of an eternal Spring morning. The colours of the flowers were of yellow, red, purple, white, and each flower seemed to glow with an aura of life energy. A gentle breeze seemed to move the grass, the trees, and the flowers. I could see real people, not grey, transparent ghosts, but real people wearing normal clothing! Their clothing was in normal colours. Real animals were moving around just ignoring me because they had no fear, because there is no fear in Heaven. Some were wild animals. Others were pets, mainly dogs, cats, and one or two horses, and obviously were there to accompany some of the people I could see. The most noticeable feeling within the feeling of love was of the profound beauty of this new "World", this other dimension that is more real than the physical earth we live on. I felt a familiarity as if I had arrived back home after an adventure into the earth plane. I didn't think to look at myself, my hands or feet, but felt my personality as my normal self, but with a profound sense of well-being, and a floating feeling with no discomfort, no pain. People were walking around yet I felt they could simply move to some other place if they wanted, through their thoughts. I could see houses like on earth, as if they were there to give a feeling of being at home to those who had passed. I could also see in the distance beautiful white buildings. I was stood in this lush green valley, and the nearest building was a thatched farmhouse. A man and his wife emerged from the farmhouse to look at me. I got the feeling that this was the same type of house they had lived in whilst in the physical world. Elsewhere in the valley people were busy, but at a steady pace. Some were gardening, tending to the flowers. I asked the Heavenly Being who was still with me where was everyone else? There should surely be many millions of people in Heaven. I could only see perhaps 30 or 40 people. The answer came instantly with a clear vision in my thoughts of many people simply resting in the white buildings in the distance. Also, that there are many valleys, and many, many different places in this very real dimension. I didn't know at the time that I would come to see many of these other places in my future role as a clairvoyant.

I noticed the sky was a hazy blue, yet an all-pervading brightness and energy emanated from above. I wondered if above the place I was visiting there was a higher place. My thoughts were instantly read! "Come, I will show you this Higher place," said this Heavenly Being. I then found myself flying upwards at speed into the sky through a barrier of white, almost like cloud, to emerge into another level of Heaven, which I now call "Second Heaven". This dimension is incredibly bright. This dimension wasn't a solid real world like the lower dimension of Heaven. It was as if I was floating in a brilliant white mist with no sign of ground or sky or distance. White radiant Beings were busy working. They could be described as Angels without wings. I knew what they were doing. They were organising everything, keeping both the dimension of Heaven, and the physical dimension supported. Above them I saw a sky of brilliant white light and felt an overwhelming and infinite energy of warmth and unconditional love. This energy was a vast loving intelligence, yet with the oneness of a person. A person who is neither a "He" nor a "She". This was the infinitely divine person who is the source of all knowledge, intelligence, meaning and purpose. I realised that this Divine Consciousness of He/ She is the Oneness, connected to the "Me" or "I" inside each one of us. This Light above me was the Source, the Creator, the centre of purity and of love and purpose. This Light above me was God. I call the Highest Heaven "Third Heaven".

I looked and received smiles of love from some of the Angelic Beings nearby. They were very busy working, looking after life, and very intent in their purpose.

The Heavenly Being who accompanied me was Spiritually Higher than the Angels for I knew that they were looking at Him with respect as a part of the Highest spiritual authority, a part of God. There was a feeling of the Heavenly Being having much, much more work to do, and that it was time for me to go. I didn't realise that from now on in my work on Earth I would catch glimpses of this place many times again. The Heavenly Being concluded the visit with a message:

"I will now leave you and I grant you the full spiritual gift of CLAIRVOYANCE to see the spiritual realm. I also pass to you the gift of spiritual discernment, to have the wisdom to discern between good and evil spirits.

Your work will be to help others with these spiritual gifts, for the world is in much need of spiritual understanding and direction".

I immediately found myself back in bed again. The time had moved from 6am to 6.30am. That half hour changed my life forever.

What happens when we pass across to the "Other Side of Life"?

The following account is fictional but incorporates most of the experiences that we can go through.

INTUITIVE CLAIRVOYANCE

John
½ marathon

John struggled for breath as he ran uphill. Sweat was pouring down his face, and he was beginning to feel exhausted. He was angry. His girlfriend, and partner of seven years, had just finished their relationship and gone off with some skinny, balding solicitor. John was nicely built and worked as a joiner but knew that his ex-partner always put money before everything else in her endless shopping sprees. Her new boyfriend was not short of money and that's what she went for.
These thoughts and feelings going around his head made him even more determined to continue running.
It was a hot June day and John was doing a half marathon to help raise money for cancer.
His father had died of a sudden heart attack when John was only 12 years old, leaving his mother to finish bringing him up. Cruel cancer had recently taken the life of his mother just six months earlier. This made it even harder to bear the loss of his girlfriend as well, but true to John's caring nature he was determined to complete the half marathon and raise some money towards supporting cancer research.
The half marathon was well organised, and at age 36 John appeared to be one of the participants in the race who should be able to complete it with relative ease.
He took a brief stop to take on some water. He drank a couple of mouthfuls then poured the remaining water over himself in a cool refreshing moment, as a waterfall of clear spring water. Then he was on his way again.
John was feeling breathless and sharp pains kept piercing his chest. His only thoughts were that he was out of condition and would book some time down at the gym starting next week.
Still, he pushed on.
Suddenly his chest was gripped, as if in a vice. He fell to the floor. He could see the ground in front of him and hear the voices of people rushing to his aid. He couldn't move.

Then all went black.

First aiders tried to resuscitate him. Paramedics arrived. The race organisers had everything in place for those who might need medical help. Rushing to John's aid were people with medical expertise. Within a couple of minutes, the blue lights of an ambulance. He was pronounced dead on arrival at hospital.

John wouldn't have known but the rare heart condition that had taken the life of his father at a young age was genetic and had now claimed a second victim.

All was black. John suddenly found himself awake. He was looking down on a scene of commotion below. An ambulance, and people milling around someone laid out on the ground. He felt free, not just free of the heaviness of a body struggling in a marathon, not just free of the pain across his chest, but free of the anger, free of the emotions that had taken over his life in recent months.

A beautiful light appeared, and he felt himself being pulled towards the light by some invisible force. Yet, he didn't feel afraid. He knew that his spirit was free and somehow all the cares and worries of his everyday life disappeared. He realised that he had died but for some reason wasn't bothered. He didn't want to go back into life. As John fell into the light a vortex in the shape of a tunnel emerged and he was drawn at high speed towards the tunnel. He found himself moving through this swirling vortex at high speed with a sense of anticipation, and a profound feeling of love surrounding him. He felt the love surrounding and protecting him as he began to perceive another light which gradually became brighter and brighter. It was the most beautiful light he had ever seen, and he felt totally at ease. There now appeared an Angel at the end of the tunnel. The vision became clearer, and he realised that his Guardian Angel was waiting to meet him.

John emerged suddenly from the vortex of the tunnel into a beautiful garden. He immediately recognised two people. "Mum…Dad, you're here to meet me!"

"We love you, so much, son," said his father. Mum smiled and gave him a hug. An embrace, that became two souls merging, through the binding love of mother and son.

"You pushed yourself too hard," his mum commented. "We were watching over you. You should have got yourself checked out for any heart problems knowing how your father passed".

John was still trying to familiarise himself with his new surroundings. It somehow didn't matter to him that his life was over. He remembered an old saying "Life is but a moment". This place he was in now was so beautiful. He felt alive, and the air he breathed was an atmosphere of love beyond description.

Mum explained that she and dad had a home here – just like the family home back in the physical world. Then his thoughts made him laugh as he said to his dad: "This place is more real than the world we lived in". Beyond the garden he could now see the family home, and in the distance were beautiful mountains. He could see the landscape of a green valley, and nearby flowers danced in a delicate breeze as their colours radiated in vivid splendour far more intense than on earth. What surprised him was that everything was real, solid, with vibrant colours. Heaven isn't a misty, intangible place. Animals are across there in Heaven, but they have no fear and simply ignored the human souls and continued grazing in the lush grass. People who cared for pets such as dogs, cats, and horses appeared to have these much-loved animals with them. The love bond between a person and that of their devoted pet shone out as a connection that spans the dimensions of earth and heaven.

John realised that Heaven was a familiar place. He had been here before. It was like coming home.

"What happens next, Mum?" was John's question after what seemed like an eternity in simply taking-in the beauty of his surroundings.

His mum replied "Well, in your case we've been told there won't be much rest. Many souls like your dad and I can spend as long as we wish just resting. However, your Guardian Angel has told us that they have an urgent mission for you. This mission will be shared by many souls who are like you".

Sleep fell upon John. He awoke to see a beautiful woman stood next to him. "Julia, Julia, is that you?"
A woman who appeared to be in her early thirties, dark flowing hair, and a flowing silver dress that shimmered like stars. Her smile was captivating. Her eyes showed a depth of love and compassion that reflected an eternal bond.
"John, I have been waiting for you for many years"
"You are, or should I say you were my wife," said John. "Oh, my beautiful Julia. I never thought I would see you again!"
John then began to feel disorientated. "I didn't have a wife, I was single. My girlfriend had just split up with me".
"Come with me," said Julia. "Those who have recently left the physical realm often feel confused. You need a time of peace and adjustment. Come, take my hand".

John joined hands with Julia and felt himself lifted up as if he weighed nothing, and was flying over beautiful valleys, houses, and a landscape so beautiful beyond any imagination. Eventually they came to rest along the shore of a lake. Contrasting shades of light shimmered in the lake before them. The movement created patterns that appeared to be alive in dancing with the joy and beauty of this place. Feelings of peace and love were overwhelming.

"I was your wife in your previous life," said Julia. "We were married for over 40 years. You died in 1970. I lived on until 1983. After I passed across to Heaven, I didn't want another life. You are my soulmate and I just wanted to wait here for you. You always were a determined soul and volunteered for another life to be born in 1989, even though you were warned that it would only be a short life because of the genetic heart defect from your earth parents."
"How come you know me as John?"
Julia laughed. "You were named John as my husband. When you

were born into a new life in 1989, I whispered in the ear of your earth parents to name you John, and fortunately they seemed to feel that was the name to give you. You will learn that those in spirit, such as ourselves, can whisper in the ear of those in the physical realm, but they don't always listen!" Julia laughed. "You never listened. I couldn't get through to you no matter how hard I tried!"

An eternity of peace, love, companionship of soulmates now seemed to pass as the two sat beside this lake of beauty and tranquillity. Time does not exist in the reality of Heaven. The only time is that of "The Now", "The Moment", "The Instant". Without the clutter of thoughts and worries about yesterday or tomorrow the time of "Now" becomes incredibly intense. John thought to himself. How he wished he had realised the value of appreciating every moment, every second of his physical life on earth. What a lesson that would have been in reducing his stress and worries, and of intensifying his everyday experience. Julia suddenly spoke: "I agree". John laughed realising that they were as one and their thoughts and feelings were shared.

John fell asleep. Julia woke him to ask if he felt ready to move on. "Our Guardian Angels have told me that we will soon have a meeting to attend," said Julia. "First, you must go to the library for your life review."

John remembered the library from his previous lives. A brilliant white building filled with books. John had lived in the digital age when books were becoming less in printed version, and everything available online. Yet the Library still looked like shelves filled with printed books.

An Angel, not his Guardian Angel, appeared and stood alongside John. "I am your Angel Guide," said the radiant soul who had the appearance of a kind but strict elderly teacher. "My name is Matthew, and it is time to review the life you have just been through."

John could see a book with his name on it.

Matthew said, "You lived a good life as a very caring person. You did make one or two mistakes. Turn to page 23, and you'll see a date of May 31st, 2010".

John opened the page. As he opened the page it became alive like a video, and then suddenly he was pulled into the scene. It was May 31st, 2010, and he had received a phone call to say his closest friend Gary was in hospital. John had been too busy with his own problems to visit him and had not fully realised how Gary had missed his friend in his time of need.

Matthew said, "You can't put things right, John. You can see and feel how hurt Gary was because you ignored his needs."

John realised that he was being taught a lesson. Life on earth is like a school. We are all there for the experiences that life throws at us, and to learn to be as caring and loving of others around us as possible even in the hardest of times.

"Don't worry," said Matthew. "You are quite an advanced soul. There were not many times in your life when you didn't show care and love for others. You can imagine how many souls find this a very harrowing time as they review lives that in some cases showed disregard and lack of love and care for people around. Where they caused deliberate hurt then they are made to feel the pain they caused, be it emotional or physical pain. Your life review has been easy, and over much more quickly than that of many others!"

As John left the Library with Matthew, Julia joined them. The Light of the Source shone above. A light that is brighter than any light in the physical universe yet does not dazzle. The energy from the Light is of pure unconditional love. John couldn't help but feel that he was a part of, and connected to everything, and that the entire spiritual universe was joined together as just one infinitely vast oneness. John suddenly knew that all human beings, and all animals have a soul energy connected to the "Oneness". John realised that the spiritual life energies that look after trees, plants, flowers, insects, and the Earth, are all connected with the "Oneness". John knew instantly that to hurt any part of the "Oneness" was like hurting oneself.

INTUITIVE CLAIRVOYANCE

John slept again. Sleep in the dimension of Heaven seemed to be a natural part of the sequence between contemplation, activity, learning, and experiencing the sheer beauty and joy of this place. He could hear music.

CHAPTER TWELVE

First Heaven

Understanding who and what we are, and why we are given life is an absolute foundation in understanding our lives so far and sorting out what the future holds for us. Understanding the System that manages life and the afterlife gives a true insight into why all events, past, present and future happen.

In unity with many religions, the clairvoyant experience is one of seeing "Heaven" as a place from which unconditional love emanates. There is definitely a "Oneness" of all soul energy culminating in the ultimate Source that I still call "God" from my Christian upbringing, and the many years spent in my adult life as an active Christian. However, the real images I see as a clairvoyant "Seeing through to Heaven" differ from most descriptions of Heaven by religious teachings.

What Does Heaven Look Like?

I name the first place we go to when we pass away from physical life "First Heaven".
It can be seen clairvoyantly as a very real, solid dimension, more real, and with a more intense experience than our physical world.

INTUITIVE CLAIRVOYANCE

There are gardens, beautiful valleys, trees, grass, flowers. Vivid Colours. Animals may appear as animals with no fear, and no aggression. People can still appear as people, although we mainly appear in our soul state as what we are – intelligent conscious energy.

Heaven allows our soul to rest after the end of physical life. One of my first discoveries, which came as a huge surprise to me, is that the first place many of us will reach is a place that may be like our home in life, and similar to the world around that we knew in life. This is to help us transition and not feel unease at what has happened in the process of so called "Death" where we find ourselves still able to see and hear. We still have feelings, and we can still think. We realise that we are still the same person with our memories intact, although worries and stress are no longer there. I will explain the reason for this later.

The following is a true account concerning the parents of a lady I was giving an Angel messages reading:

Anne came to see me. I was given a message via my Guardian Angel that her adult daughter was having a difficult time with life. This proved to be the case because her daughter's husband had recently died, suspected suicide. What came through on the reading was a message from this husband saying it was an unintentional combination of his medical condition, diabetes, and alcohol abuse that had caused his death. The following week Anne came back to see me with her daughter. The messages from the deceased husband helped ease the pain, and then a message came through from Anne's mother. I firstly gave Anne a description of her mother. My Guardian Angel helps me with a vision of the deceased person, often in great detail. As usual I gave a full description including that of hairstyle, hair colour, height and build and clothing. I was then given a vision of Anne's mother and father living in a cottage in Wales with beautiful mountain scenery nearby. This seemed strange because Anne had an obvious Yorkshire accent, and we were in East Yorkshire. Anne, however, was amazed at the description of the home in Wales. She told me that she was Welsh, and her parents had lived in the family home in Wales, as described by me, until the death of her father. Anne's mother had spent the final years of her life living with Anne In Yorkshire.

Amidst all the emotions of Anne and her daughter there was a healing process. It was only afterwards that I thought about her mother and father still together in a home that resembled their family home in Wales. The house was real, yet I knew that they were in Heaven. They were not ghosts haunting the real physical home in Wales. Heaven had given them the familiar home surroundings to be together for as long as they needed as they transition from their needs as human beings carried with them from their Earthly lives. I often find that loving parents remain in this transition place for another reason, and that is so that can still look over the lives of children or other loved ones still in physical life. We don't stay in these surroundings forever, but certainly if we wish, perhaps until our loved ones on Earth have eventually passed-on from their lives as human beings.

My logical, spiritual research indicates that there are quantum energies that connect the dimension of the physical universe and the spiritual dimension of Heaven. These energies cross back and forth between dimensions and can replicate physical landscapes and houses on Earth. I have seen this many times whilst receiving visions. I am suspicious that some of the energies theorised in quantum physics such as dark energy and dark matter might be inter-dimensional energies of enormous proportions. Physicists have been unable to identify these energies but know they exist. Perhaps it takes something beyond physical science to identify non-physical energies inter-acting with the physical universe.

A lady called Margaret came to see me for an Angel messages reading. As usual, I asked her to tell me nothing, other than confirm or deny the visions and messages that the Angels gave me.

"I see your mother who must be in spirit". Margaret replied "Yes"". I then went in to give a description of her appearance and how she had died. Margaret then asked me "Where is my mother now?". I can't ask questions, but the vision suddenly changed to an image of her deceased mother sat in a comfortable chair in her lounge, knitting and watching television. "That's exactly how my mother would spend the happy, restful times", said Margaret. I then went on to describe the lounge in more detail. I could see an unusual light fitting, a chandelier. Margaret was astonished. "No-one could know that" she said.

Again, this reading and the visions held a different slant for me as a spiritual researcher. Heaven is real and when I say that I mean a very real, solid-looking dimension. I can conclude that the mirror image of energies from the physical world can be made to produce the same familiar surroundings and objects that were around us whilst in physical life. Also, that the spiritual universe is one of unimaginable intelligence and creative ability. I then went on to relay a vision that the Angels gave me from Margaret's father. I gave a brief description of him, and how he had died of a heart attack, which Margaret confirmed as correct. I then received a further vision of him happily working under the bonnet of a red car which he seemed quite proud of. It had the appearance of a high-powered performance vehicle. The message accompanying the vision was that I was seeing what was doing in real time. Margaret was again astonished at such a clear vision and the mention of the car. "He spent all of his spare time working on cars as a hobby. The red car was his favourite!"

Visions of the Future

Visions of the Future can be massive and overwhelm the senses of vision, communication and experience. Such visions can also be faint and fleeting, but with an understanding of the System the visions are not lost.

When I see the future, my Guardian Angel gives visions of some things that will happen, and visions of some things that may or may not happen. If I see something bad, ask Heaven to "Block" it from happening, or make it somehow easier to deal with. I try to encourage good positive futures by using my own energies in that purpose.

Tunnel Vision

Deep-seated personal feelings within many of us about what we want to achieve, who we want to be, and the type of persons we want to be close to in our future.

These feelings were acquired by our soul before we were born. Those with Tunnel Vision succeed when others who don't keep hold of that focus don't succeed.

The following is a story of three brothers. As in most families the brothers all had different characters. Each had a different inner spiritual awareness. The eldest brother, John, didn't know which career to follow. His parents advised him to study for a career in accountancy because he had a natural ability to work with figures. Many years later he was earning a modest income as an accountant. The youngest brother, Sam, did well in his exam grades at school and college. He had no idea what work he wanted to do for a work career, but he had a strong work ethic and managed to earn an income as a went through life, but with several different career changes. The middle brother, Richard, didn't do particularly well in his school and college exams. Not that he wasn't intelligent. It was just that studying didn't interest him. What he did have was an inner vision that someday he would be a successful builder and property developer. With tunnel vision and determination to keep to his vision he did study for builders' qualifications. After working as an apprentice whilst he learnt his trade, he went on to establish his own building company. He kept the inner drive and determination to achieving his vision which was now to become successful with his building and property development company. He eventually became a wealthy man, and his company employed a huge number of people as it acquired new housing and office development contracts. Richard was the most successful of his brothers simply because he kept to his tunnel vision end goal, knowing exactly what he wanted to achieve in life.

Our Guardian Angels will help us to achieve our dreams, if they are realistic. Often, our inner visions are seeded in our Life Plan that was set before we were born. An important lesson is that Heaven will help us achieve our goals, our visions, if they are good and do not hurt others. We should keep to our visions with a determination to not be knocked off course because that makes it easier for Heaven to put things in place to help us along the way.

Help from the Angels

The following true account is interesting in the way that a life can be dramatically changed by working with our Guardian Angels in spiritually analysing a person's life in recent years to bring about a much brighter and positive future:

I was called to a home in Hull to give Angel message readings, to a bunch of family and friends who had booked me. Halfway through the evening I was invited into a room to read for a lady in her late sixties. I had met these friends gathered in the lounge, and then one at a time walked through to the kitchen/diner to give each a private reading. The room this lady was sat in was in between the lounge and kitchen. It was reasonably big, decorated in the flowery wallpaper so popular in the 1970s. This was the year 2006. I noticed that there was no window in the room, but it was bright and clean. She looked happy, but as I started to give her a reading, I felt very much that her life was on hold. I immediately was given a vision of a man with her in spirit who I knew was her husband. I told her this, she nodded to confirm, when I was then given a picture of a scene of a hospital bed. The same man was laid there with full life support systems attached. A doctor was in this scene looking past me at the lady I was with, asking her permission to switch off the life support. The doctor was telling her that there was nothing more the medical professionals could do. Her husband was technically brain dead, but his body was being kept alive by the machines. I gently told the lady what I was seeing. She remained calm and told me that her husband had died six years earlier. The doctor had indeed asked her permission to switch off the life support. She couldn't say yes, so went for a walk around the local streets. She had then walked back into the ward still unable to bring herself to give permission. Suddenly she just came out with the words necessary, giving permission for the life support to be switched off. The lady had remained calm whilst she told me all of this. She then became quite emotional, and said, "I murdered him. I murdered him. I have locked myself away in this room for the past six years. I haven't been out. I am looked after by my family, but I won't go out. I killed my husband." Her emotional outburst shocked me, but only momentarily. I was instantly taken back to the hospital ward. I had a bird's-eye view of her returning after her walk. I could see and hear her asking for the doctor, still undecided what to do, when suddenly her husband appeared, stood alongside her in spirit whispering in her ear "Switch off the life support. I am ok, I am free of my wrecked body, please tell him you give your permission, my love". The vision disappeared and I sat facing this emotionally distraught lady sat in front of me. I told her what I had just seen. I told her that her husband had not really been lying there in the hospital bed but was stood alongside her in spirit asking her to tell the doctor to switch off the life support.

The visions from my Guardian Angel closed as I sat opposite this lady. She slowly lifted her drooping head and stared at me eye to eye. Then a smile appeared. "You couldn't have known all of this. I now believe that my husband still exists. I did the right thing. I made the right decision."

I was then ushered out of her room to give another reading in the kitchen to a friend who had been waiting. At the end of the evening, I walked into the lounge to say goodbye to everyone. The air of excitement was electrifying. A middle-aged lady who must have been the daughter said, "Mum has told us she is no longer grieving, she is no longer blaming herself for Dad's death. She wants to get her life going again. Her first request is that I take her out shopping tomorrow. Thank you for what you have done. You have no idea what a miracle it is to see Mum wanting to live her life again." I said goodnight, feeling very much that something much bigger than me was at work. I can't perform miracles but overwhelmingly felt humbled to be a part of something so life changing.

What we may become will be shaped by our future experience

LIFE PLAN

Our Life Plan and shows how we should live our lives to gain a better place in Heaven.

Most ordinary people go to Heaven at the end of physical life. We can earn a "Better Place" in Heaven if we live our lives in a certain way.

When we say, "Better Place", then for all of us "Heaven" is a beautiful place to be. However, we are still shown the mistakes we made, and shown where we hurt others. Hurting others may have been either psychological hurt, or physical harm that we caused. Even the mostly good and caring people can accidentally or unintentionally hurt others at times, for such is the difficulty in living in our world. However, it seems to be that deliberate hurt is the most serious wrongdoing.

If we were guilty of deliberate hurt, pain, and harm against others in our life then this may be presented before us by Wise Beings in Heaven, who want us to learn. They can, if they so decide, make us intensely aware of how the hurt we caused impacted on our victims.

We should judge people by their actions, rather than what they say they might do.

Often, people may promise to help others, and promise to care, but their words never become actions.

There are some people who just "Get on" with helping others in spiritual love and care. They are so dedicated and caring towards others that they almost seem Angelic.

My research has discovered that people who show spiritual love, and physically help and care for others often have an Angel working closely with them.

In everyday life our Guardian Angel stands back from us, and helps us, when necessary, provided that we do not block our Angel through our self-centred Free Will.

When we are truly doing something that is spiritually loving and caring towards others then our Guardian Angel comes closer to help us and pass into us spiritual energies of the right kind. If we are trying to help someone who is sick, then our Guardian Angel will channel healing energies through us.

If our heart is pure, and we are dedicated in helping others, then sometimes our Angel will meld with us to become one with us. Such people may feel energised in body and in purpose. Others looking on may describe that person as "An Angel" because of their self-sacrifice and care for others.

It is not just in helping people that our Angels work. They also work through people who actively help and care for animals, for nature, and for the environment of planet Earth.

HEAVEN

Guardian Angels do not abandon us when our life is at an end. They work hard to care and comfort us towards the end of life, and then reveal themselves to us when we leave our physical body. We pass into a most beautiful light, and then find ourselves moving through a portal towards the other side of life. We move towards a place that I call "First Heaven". This is a place where most ordinary, and basically good people pass across to at the end of life's days in the physical. Most people do not have to earn their place in the Spiritual Realm of Heaven. Our main Guardian Angel meets us at the gateway to Heaven and guides us forward into the realms of Heaven.

There are other Heavens, but I feel it important to tell the world about First Heaven, because it is the place most ordinary people without strong religious beliefs go to after so called "death". If you have your own religious faith, then your religion will teach you about their Heaven.

First Heaven is surprisingly solid and much more real than the physical world around us. There are beautiful valleys, rivers, trees, and flowers in radiant bloom of most vivid colours. We are free of pain, and emotional suffering. We may realise that First Heaven is a familiar place like going home. We were there before we were born. We may be given a beautiful garden to rest. We may be given a place similar to our home to rest and feel at ease whilst we adjust to our new spiritual state, now free of our physical body with all its pain.

Loved ones who have passed before us may wait for us there, and we can find the joy of being re-united with them.

First Heaven is a "Gateway" to the further Heavens. For those with their own religious faiths then there are other "Gateways" that are described and taught by their faith.

People who were evil in life do not go to First Heaven but are sidetracked elsewhere.

In First Heaven

The Light above us is a "Sky" of gentle white light, yet whiter than any shade of white you can imagine. There is a "One" whom people may call "God", "The Source", "The Creator".

The "Oneness" of the universe, of all spiritual beings, is felt very strongly in First Heaven, a place of unconditional love. We are loved for who we are, no matter what our faults. Love is the air we breathe.

In First Heaven we can appear as we did in life with our human body. Our true self is an orb of Light and Conscious Energy, so we can also appear as that.

Communication in First Heaven is by pure thought. We instantly know what is being communicated to us, and we can talk/communicate through our thoughts.

In First Heaven we can rest if our soul needs to build up energy again after a hard life. We can also be busy and continue learning. We very much see and are accompanied by the "Guardian Angels" who helped us through life, and other Higher Angelic Beings. From First Heaven our Guardian Angels may help us look-on at those whom we love that are still in life. We can be seen by those with a gift of clairvoyance. We are not "Ghosts" when we are in First Heaven. Ghosts are something different.

LIFE REVIEW

We are given a "Life Review" in First Heaven. This is done in a loving way to see what we achieved, or to examine where we went wrong. Our lives are given to us for "Adventure", "Experience" and "Learning". The end goal is to hopefully become less self-centred, and more caring, loving and giving to others. This leads to spiritual growth.

We are shown in a loving way the mistakes and harm we may have caused to hurt others in life. We are also shown our achievements.

From this we can see that the most important lesson whilst still in life is to be loving and caring towards other people, and towards animals, nature, all of life, and the planet we live on.

Should we have done wrong it is a good idea to think about it now whilst in life, and to contemplate the errors we made. If we can try to make amends by becoming more loving and caring, this is much better than not bothering until we pass across to First Heaven.

Have you ever had a moment in your life where you could see your life clearly?

Have you ever thought: "What regrets will I carry at the end of my life? What will I wish I had done?"

A brief moment in time when we can stop in our busy lives and experience a moment of wonderful, intense clear thinking!

We may suddenly see one thing or several things that we should start to do. Things that will be positive experiences in our life that we never had time to do.

You see, in Heaven we can look back on our lives and review what we did. Heaven is a beautiful place, full of love. However, it is in

INTUITIVE CLAIRVOYANCE

this life where we can find adventure and raw experience. It is in this life that we can write a new page of our life diary each new day.

Our Guardian Angel may get through to us in moments of clear thinking, showing us things that we could be doing to maximise our life fulfilment. We should grasp these special moments with an intensity of purpose and bring changes into our life as soon as possible!

Past Lives further discussed

As a human soul we were at some point in the distant past born out of the Spiritual Oneness of the Source of all Conscious Energy. The Spiritual Dimension is a very real dimension. It is our true home. Our soul, the person whom we are, is made of conscious energy, and so the Spiritual Dimension of Heaven is our familiar home from where we came, and to where we return after each life. I believe that soul energy has been around throughout infinity, and yet gives birth to new individual souls who are given many lives in the physical universe. For most of us the recurring lives are on Earth as human beings.

The reason for human beings having many lives seems to be complex but driven by some very simple principles. These are:
To have adventure and experience.
To gain an identity. In Heaven we are an individual soul, living with other souls, and the air that we breathe is unconditional love. On Earth we are given a name, an identity, and we carve out our own path of success or failure.
The most important reason for our life is to learn to love and care for others, and for animals and nature. This is the only way that we will spiritually grow. People who have no empathy, no consideration for others will not spiritually grow, and will stay at the same soul level, or even go back to an earlier level of soul development if they have been bad to others whilst in life.

We might have started our first life 100,000 years ago and lived through many lives. Once we are at a sufficient stage in our spiritual development, we will reach a point where we don't have to go back into a life again. We will have other work to do in the Spiritual Realm.

Many of us will have started our life journey as recent as several hundred years ago. We will still have many future lives to come.

The time between lives can be several hundred years, or we can be reborn as frequent as twice per century. Many souls in Heaven have wanted to be back in life through the latter part of the 20th century, and early 21st century due to the different experience that science and technology has brought about. They all want the experience of travel by car and plane, computers, TV, mobile phones, and a less physical struggle compared with the primitive rural lives they might have had in the past. That is why there are over seven billion people alive today.

An interesting thing can be pointed out: Those who don't care about the planet and climate change don't realise that future generations will probably include a reincarnated life for them, so they will also suffer as reborn souls.

There are many true accounts of readings that I have given concerning how our past lives affect our present life.

Kelly (not her real name) came to me for an Angel message reading. Without her saying anything I was immediately given a message from the Angels that she had at least three long-term relationships that had ended badly. I also could see that she presently didn't have a close relationship.

Kelly immediately responded by saying "You are correct. Why does this always happen to me? Why can't I have a long-term, happy relationship?"

I added to my reading by seeing that her first relationship by marriage was very brutal. She had been subject to mental and physical abuse. She confirmed that, and almost broke down in tears.

I knew I had to get to the cause of these recurring relationship problems, and I sensed the Angels giving me visions on her immediate past life. I saw that she had been a woman (sometimes we have different genders in different lives), and that she had been married happily for over forty years. Her marriage in this past life was full of love, and she had been a mother to several children. I then saw a vision of her husband in this past life and compared it with the vision of her three failed relationships in this life. That's the answer! In this life she had instinctively been attracted to men with similar appearance, similar physical qualities to her husband in the past lives. This instinctive attraction had over-ridden the personality problems of her three failed relationships who had all treated her badly and each hurt her in their own way.

I told her the conclusions that this Life Plan reading had given. She sat there for a minute, saying nothing, and absorbing what I had said. "You are right," she said. "It all makes sense!"

I advised her to look at the personal, character qualities of any future partner. Some weeks later I saw her again. She is now in another relationship with a man she says has a pleasant character and is genuinely caring. She seems really happy.

Our Life Plan was determined in Heaven before we were born.

We will emerge from a life on Earth back in our familiar home of Heaven having been shaped by our most recent life, and still carrying our experiences from previous lives.

We will have gained yet another identity, a new name, in our last life. We will need a period of adjustment, a period of orientation now we are back in the spiritual realm of Heaven.

Most souls go to a place that I name "First Heaven". I have already gone into further detail of First Heaven elsewhere in this book, but it is best described as a place with similarities to Earth. There are beautiful flowers, trees, and all of nature resplendent in a landscape of valleys, vivid green grass, streams, and even houses. People may appear as they did in life, usually in middle age or younger. Our Guardian Angel accompanies us during this time,

when we are also given a Life Review to see our life, almost like a video. During the Life Review will we see the good things that we did, our mistakes, and the hurt we may have caused others.
It also happens that in addition to adventure and experience during our physical life we are also measured on our ability to love and care for others, including all of life in animals and nature.

In First Heaven we can look-on at loved ones who are still alive in the physical. This is when people, such as me, can make a connection and bring messages. Such connection is via Guardian Angels. The word Angel interprets as "Messenger".
After a long period of time in First Heaven (although there is no such thing as time across there, only the moment of "Now"), we move on towards further learning and experience in other areas of Heaven. We will re-unite with our true soulmates who were born as a soul at the same time as ourselves. We may talk to each other to share our individual experiences in our lives on Earth. We may have met at least one of our soulmates in life, been a friend with one of them, or even shared a life as a partner or family member with a soulmate.

At some point we will be encouraged to move forward and agree to being born again into another life as a human being. This isn't forced on us, especially if our previous life was painful or traumatic. Our soul is given a chance to rest and rebuild our soul energy.
Before we go into a new life our Life Plan is drawn up by our Guardian Angel, together with other wise beings. These beings are like people, but spiritual beings who have lived through many lives and are now teachers.
Our Life Plan will address our character deficits from a perspective of developing our soul to be more loving and caring of others whilst in life. Our Life Plan can build-in the interests we may wish to develop, the work we might do, and the people we are destined to meet.
Life Plans will always include Life Challenges which are never easy

but are not meant to cause personal suffering.

Free Will is destined to influence our day-to-day decisions, yet the major events and people we are destined to meet on our Life Plan will still happen, no matter what our free will decisions do to our lives.

Some souls volunteer for a life where they will have some physical disability, or a particularly tough life. This is because our souls learn more rapidly and spiritually develop to a higher level through hardship and struggle. If we are still able to be caring and loving towards others when our life is tough then we are truly spiritually bigger and stronger, and that's what Heaven seems to want of us.

LIFE PLAN MESSAGES

Much of our life up to now, our present, and our future, was planned-out in Heaven before we were born.

With messages and visions from my Angel Guide I scan the past lives of a person, and then move on to visions of the time in Heaven when their Life Plan for this life was being worked out and drawn up.

I'll give you a true example:

Richard came to me for a Life Plan reading. He had been through a divorce and was concerned for his children so shared custody with his ex-wife.

He was in some ways lonely, and needed to find a new friendship, a new partner, but his divorce had meant giving his home up to his ex-wife, and short of money for moving on, and no time for finding new friends.

I started by seeing if the Angels would give me visions of his past lives. When I work with the Angels in this way, I mainly pick up feelings of how a person was in past lives. I could see he had been quite selfish in his past lives and had only thought about his own needs. This had meant that others around him had been psychologically hurt by his lack of care.

Then came the Life Review whilst in Heaven before his present life. I could see that being selfish had held back his spiritual growth. He had agreed with the wise ones who put together his Life Plan that he would try to be more caring of others next time.

I was then given visions of his life up to now. I could see that he had clashed with his ex-wife because she was and is very self-centred. He wanted to be there for his children in sharing custody. He seemed determined to work hard at being genuinely caring, not putting himself first.

I explained the Angel messages to him, and he agreed with the findings.

I further explained that he was going through a period of his life when the interests of the children, and the needs of the children to still have a caring father, were more important than his own personal wishes, and he agreed.

Looking to the future for him I could see a vision of a future partner, an improved financial position and new home. The timeline of the vision coming to fruition was, however, several years hence. He said he was happy at that. He felt justified in his present lifestyle of some self-sacrifice for the benefit of his children and was so impressed at the accuracy of the reading that he felt he could now feel less anxious about his present life.

I saw him several times, and each time he felt he was becoming spiritually calmer, stronger and wiser, and that he was less depressed and coping with everyday life much better.

What about things that happen to people to prevent life fulfilment?

Wars, accidents, pandemics, and other events that lead to human severe suffering are not usually on a person's Life Plan. Lives cut short by such tragedies see a soul return to Heaven earlier than planned.

The first process in Heaven is to give a soul rest, counselling, and a

chance to rejuvenate their soul energies. A Life Plan can be picked up again, perhaps modified, and made ready for a new life once a person feels ready to enter another life.
Heaven is always viewed as a safe retreat for us, a familiar home where we truly belong. However, the lack of any memory of Heaven, combined with the cold, painful hardships of life leave us as human beings reluctant to accept that those in Heaven exist, let alone truly love us.
Also, many people have a terrific passion for life, and work hard towards achieving success in education, sport, music, art, and business. In addition, many people build up a family, and life seems at its most harsh when any tragedy strikes.

The Life Challenges that are set for us on our Life Plan are not life tragedies. Also, no matter whom we are as a soul our Life Plan may be severely restricted by others around. We may care for someone with a disability for many years and put our own dreams aside. This is where we surrender our free will to help others. This is of course spiritually positive and will help our continued soul development.
We may live in a society that restricts personal freedoms, or we might find ourselves poor in an affluent society where money rules. Both are examples of how our Life Plan might not attain fulfilment.

It is when I am giving a person detail of their current and past life situation that I often find that they want to know more about what the future holds for them.
I can move into a Life Plan reading seamlessly, and very quickly look at their past live. I ask my Guardian Angel specific questions, in my mind thoughts, concerning the Life Plan of my client. My Guardian Angel works with the Angels that accompany my client. The questions I ask can typically include: Is the unfair and difficult time in my client's life now at an end? What better future can my client have? What are the hopes and dreams of my client, and will these be achieved in the future?

At this point on the reading assessment, I can explain to the client all that I have been given in clairvoyant messages and visions. I then "Block" any unwanted things that could happen in my client's future should he or she simply carry on as they are with life. I then explain to the client the positive things that will come into their life, and as I explain the good things, such as a new friend, a new job or career, a new home, or perhaps fulfilment in sport, art, or music, I can see that a process is underway of changing their future Life Path for the better.

The following is a true case:

Linda came to see me. I could see her deceased mother in spirit. The love bond between them was strong and I brought through a lot of information from her deceased mother, including a message to not feel guilty for not being by her side when she unexpectedly passed. This message was received emotionally by Linda who was overjoyed to have re-united with her mother for those few minutes. I might have ended the reading there, but I was seeing visions of her life and that she wasn't completely happy. She was happily married with two children but couldn't understand why she felt deep-down unhappy.

I reviewed her past life where I picked-up that she had been a musician, playing the piano, and her best friend in her previous life, a female, had been one of her soulmates who was also a musician. I reviewed her life up to now, and she had money, a happy family, everything most people would want, but hadn't given herself any space for her own interests, the main one of which was music.

I then asked for visions of her Life Plan. I could see that if she took up music as a hobby and took time to learn a musical instrument then she would find long-term fulfilment and she would also meet her sou-mate again, and a close friendship would happen.

Linda was amazed at the revelations from her Angel messages Life Plan reading, and excited to be on a new path of life fulfilment, now very determined to allow herself time for her own passion in music.

CHAPTER THIRTEEN

The Past and Future are linked

When I am giving an Angel messages reading, I am often given visions of future positive events. These are always impressive, but I personally would often feel that I could help people more. Angel readings are meant to help people move forward with their lives in a positive way.

I always sense other underlying factors at play in a person's past, present, and future life. Finding out what these factors are can help give a much clearer view of our individual futures.

When giving someone a reading I often see that there could be a choice of futures. I needed to know what clairvoyant guidance I could give someone to help them live a more positive, happier and fulfilling future.

I was a Christian until aged 55. I thought that the messages and spiritual visions from the Angels were religious experiences, even though many years of spiritual research were revealing a different picture to the teachings of my faith. Most Christian faiths disapprove of anyone having visions, and I eventually had to be sincere to myself in quietly stepping down from my Christian work which at that time was as a trainee Methodist preacher.

I now believe that we all have experienced many past lives. Christian beliefs are in our one life only, and to strive towards salvation through our beliefs, actions and deeds in this life.

Although I now know that we, as an eternal soul, have many lives, I am still passionate about living this life as if it were the only life that we have.

Past Lives can sometimes be identified through a personal hypnotherapy consultation.

Some clairvoyants, including myself, can pick up on a person's immediate past life, and even some previous past lives.

Our past lives have helped make us into the person we are in this life and continue to influence our present life in many ways.

Inner feelings that we can't explain could be caused by a previous past life.

The following is a true account, but with the person's name changed.

I gave Katie an Angel messages reading. I had never met her before, and she appeared to be around the age of 60 years. I immediately felt the pain of a recently broken relationship, and she confirmed that as being correct.

I asked her to say nothing and told her that I could see that she has three adult children, and that the father was from an earlier relationship break-up.

I was given a vision of a partner in spirit, with her, and he was very apologetic concerning his behaviour in the latter part of their relationship.

Katie confirmed that she had been through three marriages, and that all three husbands had turned to drinking excess alcohol, and became selfish, and aggressive. She had to pull away from each of the marriages.

"Why does this always happen to me!" came as an outburst from Katie.

The partner who had died was with her in spirit, and confirmed that he had been her second husband, and after 14 years of happy marriage had suffered a major personality change after becoming an alcoholic.

INTUITIVE CLAIRVOYANCE

He was sorry for his selfish behaviour. I passed this message on to Katie, and she then told me that her marriage with him had been the "Best".

I couldn't explain "Why this is always happening to her" in an immediate spiritual assessment.
However, my Guardian Angel started to give me visions of Katie's past life. She had been happily married in her past life, and I began to see that in her present life she had been attracted to men with similar looks to her husband in her past life. She had just "Felt" that a prospective partner was right for her, based on his looks, not knowing why, and disregarding a future partner's character defects.

Being a different gender in a past life can be an explanation for our feelings in this life

The following is a true account, but with her name changed.

Linda, age mid-twenties, came to see me for an Angel messages reading. She was, and is, openly a lesbian, and admitted that her true feelings had emerged after having some unpleasant relationships with men in her teenage years.
Linda had a massive anger problem and felt that she couldn't conform with school and education when younger and was now unemployed and unable to focus on a career.
She was looking for a loving relationship with another woman, but as yet was unable to find true happiness.
At first the Angel messages for her gave nothing concerning her personal difficulties, only that her grandfather gave some simple messages.
Suddenly, my Guardian Angel gave me a vision of a young man, aged 19 years, in a battle. It was World War Two, and he was fighting alongside his comrades when they were hit by an artillery shell. The first experience he had was of his soul being thrown out of his body, and himself in spirit being pulled into the Light of Heaven.

We leave anger and stress behind before we reach Heaven. Even so, his regret at having his life cut short of not experiencing a long and loving relationship with a girlfriend carried in his memory.

Once reborn into a new life in the 1990s, as a female, named Linda, he had lost his memory of his immediate past life. However, the anger re-emerged, and his search for a loving female relationship eventually started to dominate him, now as Linda.

Upon communicating this vision to Linda, she immediately felt that at last there was an explanation for her anger, and for not being interested in a career. She felt that she had at last realised who she was and is. She will continue looking for a happy, loving, lesbian relationship, and hopefully find some employment career, now knowing how her past life has affected her present life in such a big way.

As we progress through many lives we naturally want to ask: "Why do we have lots of lives?
Living lives for the adventure and experience are certainly some of the main reasons.

Those in Heaven see the Grand Purpose of our lives as becoming more caring and loving towards others, animals, nature, and our beautiful planet, and being less self-centred.

It would seem as though younger souls are naturally more self-centred, and more mature souls become more loving and caring to others.

I have considered this carefully in my research over many years and come to the conclusion that for Heaven to survive, those souls dwelling there must be loving and caring to each other. It's a feeling of Oneness.

This feeling of Oneness is so strong in Heaven that as we become aware of how we hurt others, and hurt nature, then we start to realise that we are equally hurting ourselves.

Planet Earth has many younger souls. This is self-evident in self-centred behaviour, and lack of empathy towards others, that is widespread.

Mature souls are more loving and caring. They may sacrifice many of their own worldly pleasures to help others, and nature.

So, our present and future life is being determined by our spiritual progress. This can be identified clairvoyantly.

Between Lives – Life Review and our next life

At the end of each life our soul, the person that we may call "I" or "Me", leaves our physical body, and returns home to Heaven.

After many years of giving Angel message readings, I realise that we carry across there not only our character, but also our memories.

When reading to connect with someone who suffered from dementia, I find that spiritually retained memories only go as recent as immediately prior to the onset of their dementia.

We do not carry serious emotions, stress, anger, worry, or sorrow across with us. We leave these behind as we find ourselves entering the spiritual realm of pure, unconditional love.

When we leave our physical body, we will find ourselves seeing our Guardian Angel, probably for the first time. Our Guardian Angel will appear as a person, but radiant with soul energy. We will not feel afraid, but instinctively know that this is a Being of love.

Most people, most souls, pass across to Heaven after their physical life is at an end.

I call this place "First Heaven" because it is the first place we travel to.

First Heaven is very real and solid. The immense beauty and vivid colours are beyond description.

There are fields, trees, flowers, rivers and lakes. There may also be homes, similar to a home where a soul may have lived on Earth.

I describe First Heaven in more detail elsewhere in this book. However, we will have many things to do. These include re-uniting with our soulmates, a Life Review, looking at our Life Lessons and spending time with Wise Beings in the Afterlife who will assess our spiritual progress.

Planning our next life

Our next life is actually planned in Heaven before we are reborn. We will be aware of our future Life Plan and know the reasons why our future life will hold Life Lessons.

When we are reborn, the conscious memory of our time in Heaven is deliberately erased. However, our Guardian Angels know our Life Plan, and by becoming more aware of our Guardian Angels, and how they communicate through our feelings, we can be more in touch with understanding the reasons for our life experience in the past and present and obtain a glimpse of our future Life Plan events yet to happen.

Working with my Guardian Angel, I can pick up messages and visions of our future Life Plan events clairvoyantly.

Past Life behaviour will determine some of our present life experiences

Whilst in Heaven we will at some point experience a Life Review. This usually happens soon after our passing.

Our Life Review is in the presence of our Guardian Angel, and Higher Spiritual Beings, often appearing in human form.

A lot of emphasis is given on how much we helped others in our lives. This is classed as good and positive.

In situations where we were totally self-centred in our behaviour towards others, these situations will be brought to our attention. If we were lacking in empathy, and in situations where we deliberately hurt others emotionally or physically, then this is looked on as bad behaviour. We can be shown life situations in our life that has passed as if reliving them in real time, but this time feeling the hurt we may have caused.

How are we punished for bad behaviour?

Punishment isn't the correct way of describing the outcome of our bad behaviour. Heaven is a place of unconditional love and safety for all who make it there, and most souls do reach Heaven successfully.

After our Life Review, there is a realisation at a spiritual level of shared responsibility for each other. A feeling of "Oneness" of all souls, and that if we hurt another soul, we are also hurting ourselves.

We eventually will volunteer for another life where we might agree to be a victim of someone who treats us badly, just as we hurt others in the past. This would be to give us an experience where we can learn. Our souls often grow more quickly in positive ways during hard times in life.

If we can endure our own difficult life, and yet still be caring towards others, then we are truly growing spiritually.

So, it can be seen that our past lives, followed by our Life Plan mapped out in Heaven, would have had a significant role to play in our current life. This often explains why some people's lives seem to have been harder than others.

The good news is that if we sense our Guardian Angel we can learn to identify "Life challenges" set before we were born.

For all of us, learning to be closer to our Guardian Angels can help us "Feel" that we know our Life challenges.

Can the Life challenges be avoided in the future and a person's life changed for the better? *Absolutely, yes!* **Our future after this life – will be affected by our behaviour in this life**

CHAPTER FOURTEEN

LIFE AS A PERSON SEEING ANGELS

This chapter is written to explain further what I see and experience.

There is no scientific evidence of the eternal spiritual soul that we all are and have. It is the person inside whom we call "I" or "Me". That person inside has an eternal existence beyond our physical life.

Everything spiritual, including our soul, is of another dimension. That is why physical science cannot detect our soul and cannot detect Heaven.

Within ourselves, we are a soul of conscious, intelligent energy made of the same stuff as the energies of Heaven. Heaven is our true familiar home where we came from, and to where we return. The human brain is most amazing. The brain has within the ability to link and meld with our soul energy. The neurons firing within the brain create energies that communicate with our soul energy so perfectly that we feel as one with our human body born into the physical world of Earth. The brain is a link with both the dimension of Heaven and Earth. Perhaps future discoveries of how this link works might provide some scientific evidence of the spiritual dimension.

What do I experience as a person Sensing Angels?
Well, firstly I try to ground myself in everyday life. I am a qualified

accountant and have always worked hard in my career. I have hobbies and interests, and a passion for my main interest – music. Sending Angels is something that I can switch-on when my mind turns to it.

When I am giving someone a reading, I sense their Guardian Angel communicating with my Guardian Angel. It is they who enable the readings to happen. I am given visions as images of people who have passed, of scenes in someone's life, of landscapes, homes, cars, and almost anything. The visions are always of relevance to the person I am helping through the reading. I also receive information, either as a sudden voice when I am given a name, or a sudden "knowingness".

What I do find consistently is that the readings only occur where there is a bond of love, family, or friendship, between the person in front of me and the person in spirit.

Throughout my life I have also been given visions of other things:

I can see across to Heaven.
The place I see is a place I call "First Heaven". This is because this is the first place we go to after we pass across from our physical life.

I can see people who are in spirit where there is a love or friendship connection.

I can receive messages via my Guardian Angel in the form of visions, and messages as a voice or "Sudden knowingness".

I can see the Guardian Angels of people and I can communicate with them.

I can see that Angels respond to our prayers to God. The Angels work on the instructions and in the purpose of God.

I can see Angels bringing healing to people. I can see the different colours of the energies Angels channel when bringing healing. I can help people myself in channelling healing from the Angels.

I can see Life Plans, and some of a person's future. The future is also determined by our free will.

I can see Angels working in nature.

I can see, feel, and know the meaning of life.

Angels help in the following ways: Angels speak to us through our intuition. Have you ever struggled with a problem, unable to find an answer, then suddenly the answer is there? Have you ever been overwhelmed by stress and worry, and then somehow you work through the situation? Have you ever had a gut feeling that you shouldn't go somewhere, and later discover that you are glad you listened to your intuition? Maybe you didn't listen to your intuition and regretted doing something? Your Guardian Angel helps you through your intuition. There is no language, just an instant awareness of what we should or shouldn't do by a form of telepathy which we don't acknowledge because we don't realise that we are being helped. In some people the fine tuning of their intuition can lead to an individual becoming in some ways clairvoyant. If we pray to God for healing, then a Healing Angel will help bring healing directly to the person suffering, both spiritually, and through those working to help medically.

Angels can be with us to give us STRENGTH. Both physical, and emotional strength.

A Prayer to God is essential. Angels can be with us to guide us through life's problems and difficulties.

Angels helping us in our daily lives can only be appreciated if we believe in God and the Angels.

A word of caution: Angels rarely communicate as a voice in your head unless to give a sudden warning of imminent danger. A voice in your head is not allowed because a voice telling us what to do would go against our "Free Will" to live our lives as we choose. Also, an Angel of God would never be a nuisance by bothering you in ways you don't want. Angels of God certainly never guide us with bad thoughts.

Angels help all of us as we near the end of life, and when we pass across to Heaven.

I have had an account from a nurse who has worked in the resuscitation ward of hospital. She informed me that whenever she saw an Angel at the bed head of a patient, she knew the patient was more likely to die. The doctors and her would inevitably have a more difficult time, but often still saved the life of such patients.

Angels who bring healing. A prayer to God can bring direct healing help through the Angels and help by bringing professional medical attention.

Angels to provide our basic needs of food, clothing, a friend to talk to.

What do you really want out of life? What do you need most to achieve fulfilment? Well. The Angels won't help you win the lottery, but they can offer a tremendous amount of help in achieving our goals, and fulfilment in life. What do we need to do? Well, the starting point is simply to be open-minded to a belief in Angels!

Life changing experiences

Most life-changing experiences are quiet, personal ones. Earlier in the book I described how I felt a Guardian Angel with me when I was near death in hospital with asthma. However, as I grew older, into my teens, as with any normal teenager my mind forgot about spiritual experiences from my infancy. My subsequent life-changing experiences were quiet, personal ones. I wasn't suddenly going to change the world overnight by bringing to the world my vision, and a new way of life. No, the world doesn't change. Life hopefully continues. We should count each day as a blessing. We should think of the things we have in this life and be thankful. We should try not to become too depressed or consume ourselves with jealousy because of things we don't have. Earlier in the book I described a very real experience of a vision and a spiritual journey given to me by an Archangel on 1stMay, 1999. Over the weeks and months following my journey into Heaven I experienced visions of Light many times. I still do, to this day. When the moments are more intense, I see the face of the Heavenly Being. His eyes always draw my attention. They have depths of infinite wisdom, understanding and unconditional love. Immediately after my journey to Heaven I knew I was being prepared to do some kind of spiritual work to help others. I could ask in my thoughts almost any question about the meaning of life, and the answer would be given to me. I was on a rapid learning curve. I learnt the power of prayer, and that non selfish prayers to God are listened to and answered, but not always with the answer we want!

CONCLUSION

The Afterlife of Heaven is real, and the Angels in Heaven are working constantly through the many people who work in genuine love and care for others, for nature and for planet Earth.

Those who choose to learn some clairvoyant skills through closer awareness and partnership with our Guardian Angels, can discover personal empowerment to be guided by Heaven in every aspect of their lives.

I urge the world to believe that we are truly spiritual children of God and that we can learn to recognise and act on our individual callings to do some good in this world. Together we can save planet Earth from the worst consequences of climate change. Heaven is real and Angels are real. Individually we can learn to sense our Guardian Angels so that we can be guided by them to stay safe, and work towards a happier and fulfilling future. Sensing the Angels can truly bring miracles into our lives.

Should anyone wish to further advance their clairvoyant ability, this is progressed by personal guidance and tuition. To enquire, please see my website: intuitionxyz.com or contact me by email: spirtualresearchx@outlook.com

Copyright Robert Mason 2023

Printed in Great Britain
by Amazon